RETURN TO FORT APACHE

APACHE

Memoir of an NYPD Captain

TOM WALKER

iUniverse, Inc.
Bloomington

Return to Fort Apache
Memoir of an NYPD Captain

iUniverse books may be ordered through booksellers or by contacting:

iUniverse
1663 Liberty Drive
Bloomington, IN 47403
www.iuniverse.com
1-800-Authors (1-800-288-4677)

ISBN: 978-1-4620-2049-2 (sc)
ISBN: 978-1-4620-2051-5 (hc)
ISBN: 978-1-4620-2050-8 (e)

Library of Congress Control Number: 2011908886

Printed in the United States of America

iUniverse rev. date: 06/15/2011

DEDICATION

This book is dedicated to the men and women I've served with both as a lieutenant and as a captain in the Four-one Precinct. Many are memorialized in the book and in Appendix A. I wish I could tell you a little something about each of them. Obviously, I can't. Maybe, after you read this book, you will understand why these guys and gals are forever in my heart.

PREFACE

This is a book that wasn't going to be written. I wrote a book, "Fort Apache – Life and Death in New York's Most Violent Precinct" about my adventures as a lieutenant in the South Bronx's Four-one Precinct in 1971. We had more murders in that one New York City precinct that year than did the entire city of San Francisco.

When I was promoted to captain in 1972 I left the Four-one, but I would return in 1974 prior to the book's publication.

The book caused so much consternation and concern within the police department, the community and in my own home (numerous death threats), that any thought of doing a sequel was quickly sublimated.

Then, in January 2011, the N.Y.C. Police Department released some startling statistics. In 1971, the police killed 93 people and wounded 221. In 2010, the police killed 8 people and wounded 16.

In a sense, the N.Y.P.D. was throwing me and the thousands of cops of that era under the bus. Yes, we are proud of what the city and N.Y.P.D. have accomplished in 40 years.

But it took more than just improvements in police tactics and equipment to garner such achievements. It took enlightened city leadership, community education, law abiding citizens, and too many dead and wounded cops to slow down the violence. Where is the notation that 15 police officers died in the line of duty in 1971— shot, stabbed, and assassinated. One of those killed was Four-one Precinct Detective

Joseph Picciano. One of the 93 people killed that year by the police was Joe's killer shot by Joe's partner, Bill Lally. And so it went.

We didn't shoot people without justification. Yes, we made mistakes, but there were over 2,000 citizens of New York City killed that year. I counted 123 of those murders in Fort Apache (some might have been reclassified). The Four-one Precinct had the most crime, its cops were the most shot at in the country, the most assaulted, and the most ignored by the department brass. The entire city was a killing field.

But the war didn't end in the year 1971. So let me take you back, beyond that year, and tell you the rest of the story. The story of my Return to Fort Apache.

PROLOGUE

▼

It was on a hot muggy July night in the mid 70's that I decided to quit the N.Y.C. Police Department. Cynicism had a lot to do with it. I was the Duty Captain that night. It was my job to respond to any serious incident – "Unusuals" in P.D. parlance – investigate and write up a report with recommendations, if necessary, to the Chief Inspector. I was in the Four – O Precinct signing the blotter to document a required visit when my chauffeur, Sal, burst into the muster room.

"Cap, we got a shooting, the Four – three", he yelled.

I acknowledged his shout by nodding slowly. Not again, I thought. Every time I catch borough duty somebody gets killed. "Who got shot?" I asked.

Sal was wiggling, trying to separate his wet uniform shirt from his back.

"A perp – cop shot a perp – sounds bad," he offered.

We were on our way. I checked with the radio dispatcher for the exact location.

"Behind a garage at 1520 Blackrock Avenue," cracked the radio. "Bus on the way – Four – three sergeant two minutes away."

"E.T.A. is 5 minutes," I replied.

I checked the speedometer. Sal was hitting 70 MPH heading north on Bruckner Blvd. He swerved into the center lane to avoid a stream of water directed at us from an open hydrant by some distempered kids.

"Take it easy Sal. I want to get there in one piece."

"Nervous, huh Cap?" Sal kidded.

"No, experience Sal. I already have 200 hundred stitches in my head from turning over in one of these bombs."

The speedometer moved back toward 60 MPH. Sometimes five minutes seems like an eternity. Especially if your radio is on a different frequency from those involved in the action. The radio dispatcher kept us informed as we moved toward Blackrock Avenue.

"Four – three Sergeant on the scene."

Some seconds later. "E.M.S. on scene."

And finally, "E.M.S. says the kid is D.O.A."

I winced – a kid. I had five children. I sensed the horror and agony that this news would bring to a mother, father, a family. In retrospect, I now know that it is impossible to truly imagine that horror until it happens to you. It's worse than anything you can imagine. But I didn't know that then – my daughter Cathy hadn't contracted Juvenile diabetes yet – she was still alive.

I walked toward the garage behind the house on Blackrock Avenue. In the distance sirens wailed, horns honked and alarms clanged. It was that kind of night in the South Bronx. A group of 20 hushed people – cops, medics, and neighborhood folks, stood like garden statues under the portable lights set up by emergency service to illuminate the deadly scene. It was eerie – surreal. These scenes always are until you see the body. Then, it's all too real.

The young man lay between the garage and a property defining rock wall. The smell of gunpowder still lingered about the body. There wasn't the hint of a breeze. I pointed my flashlight at the figure. He had a healthy strong body; a white boy; probably Italian. I moved the light toward his face. It was a nice face. Then I saw it. My heart sank – I drew a deep breathe – my cheeks quivered. It was a tear. The poor bastard had a tear on his cheek. I can be a tough son-of-a-bitch cop when needed, but before anything, before everything, I'm a human being – a father, a husband, a son. My soul was pierced. I don't know why I did it. It wasn't a conscious act. It caused murmurs from those assembled. I bent over the young man and with my folded white handkerchief gently wiped the tear from his cheek. I then kissed the handkerchief and slid it into the boy's pants pocket. Good police procedure? No, but the tear belonged to this young man. It was his last conscious act. It was his. I wanted him to have it. Too much had been taken from him already.

I was tired. Too many young people murdered, too many seniors murdered, too many shootings, too many young cops killed, too many young cops wounded, too much killing. But that's not what made up my mind to quit. That came later – at the station house. Right now, I had a job to do – find out what happened and why! I slowly pieced it together.

It had started as a joy ride – steal a car, take it for a ride, pick up some girls and then dump the car. The three boys were spotted dumping the car. It had been reported stolen. Each boy fled in a different direction – one into St. Raymond's Cemetery, one down Tremont Avenue and the last one toward Blackrock Avenue. The first two were easily caught. Number three was an athlete – he could run. He disappeared behind the stucco house on Blackrock. Other responding officers reported by radio that the boy hadn't crossed the adjoining street. P.O. Pace paused to listen – to hear a twig or heavy breathing. Pace heard a noise behind the garage. "Come out you little M.F.", he yelled repeatedly. There was no movement. Pace, gun at the ready, inched his way toward the rear of the garage and peeked behind it. The kid was trying to hide. Pace reported that he lost his balance and fell as he reached for the kid, struck his gun hand against the garage and accidently discharged one shot which pierced the youngster's heart. An accident. A fuckin' accident. Did I believe the cop? It was obvious that Pace's hand was badly bruised. There was nothing to indicate he was lying – nothing. There weren't any witnesses. The physics of the situation was logical. Everything supported Pace's story and so would my report to the Chief Inspector. But, that aside, I was still seething. A kid died unnecessarily. Sure, the kid had done a stupid thing, an illegal thing but nothing to die for. You think of your own boys at times like these. That could be your 16 year old son behind that garage. Even good kids do stupid things once in a while. And that's what added to my frustration that night. There was no good answer. No good rationalization. How could I respond to a mother's plaintiff cry, "Why? Why, my son?"

But even that, the fact that I didn't have a good answer to an unanswerable question, wasn't the reason I decided to quit. I made my decision sitting in the Captain's office at the Four – three stationhouse.

I puffed on a TeAmo cigar as I awaited the arrival of the night duty assistant district attorney.

Statements would be taken from all the living participants of note. The court stenographer had arrived and was setting up his equipment. The homicide detective assigned to the case was shifting a desk and carefully arranging the chairs so we all could hear the interrogations. Inspector Ciccotelli bounded through the door.

"Bad kid, bad kid", he pronounced. "Smoked pot I hear. Had a fight with a teacher too.

"Definitely capital offenses", I moaned. "An accident is an accident. Can't we let it at that?"

Ciccotelli, a round man of Italian extraction, ignored me. He always did. He was on his way up the ladder of command. I was barely holding on to it.

The phone rang. The detective picked it up. It was super Chief Thomas Mitchelson. Mitchelson was one of the top five bosses in the department – The highest ranking black. The detective held the phone in the air. "The chief wants to talk to the Duty Captain", he said.

Before I could move, Inspector Ciccotelli had seized the phone. I could only hear one side of the conversation. It went like this:

"Right Chief, Right Chief."

"Yeah, I'm sure you've been there before Chief."

"Yeah, bad kid. Drugs – assault."

"Yeah, clean shooting. Accidental."

"Thanks Chief, I'll handle it."

"Goodnight Chief."

Ciccotelli, an Italian, had just used the death of a 16 year old Italian kid to make political points with Chief Mitchelson. In effect he was saying, "Chief, you had to take it like a man when some black kid was killed, well I can take it too." It was the ultimate in cynicism.

It was the last straw. The so-called, "Straw that broke the Camel's back."

I no longer wished to serve under men like these. It was time, I decided that night, to pack it in, to retire.

But that's the end of the story. Before I reached the last straw there were many straws accumulated before, during and after my Return to Fort Apache.

CHAPTER 1

▼

On May 21, 1971, the same day Police Officers Piagentini and Jones were assassinated in the 32nd Precinct in Harlem, I arrived at the Four-one Precinct as a newly promoted lieutenant.

I got lucky and was able to take the civil service test for captain shortly thereafter. I scored well and was promoted to captain in August of 1972. The Police Commission decided that I needed a change of venue.

My move to the Five-O, in the Riverdale section of the Bronx, meant a jump back. It was peaceful; its streets wound around the hills that make the Hudson so beautiful, and in the summer, trees shrouded the sidewalk with cool shade. I left the South Bronx I had come to love, the Bronx of many textured faces, streets swollen with life, throbbing with voices, change jangling in pockets, shoes moving to the next exciting block.

The last time I saw the Four-one, few people recognized me. I did not find that fact troublesome. I rested easily in my guise as policeman. And I felt there was nothing in the past at the Four-one that should cause me foreboding. My job was done in this special hell. I simply came back to pick up my last paycheck. Parking was still tough, but I managed to find a spot near the stationhouse. As in the past two summers, the heat lay everywhere and only the young showed signs of energy as they romped through open hydrants. I dodged them and the cars that stood on stilts made of metal milk crates. Rust seemed to be the only timepiece suited for this neighborhood – rust and occasional blotches of blood. I tried but I could not ignore Simpson Street.

Across from the Fort, a small group of excited people gathered. They lacked the boisterousness that marked many crowds. A patrolman named Bill Smyth stood among them, unthreatened. In the center of the crowd lay a three-year-old boy. He had apparently fallen from a fifth-floor window and been impaled on the prongs of a wrought iron fence. When I arrived, he still struggled to free himself, but it was too late.

How it happened, no one will know. Faces always lined these windows, watching the precinct. I had probably seen this kid a hundred times, I thought, as Bill Smyth and the ambulance attendant carefully extricated him and placed him on a stretcher. I stood there, taller than most of the crowd. The sun reddened my complexion and didn't tan it. I was very separate from these people. Yet, after these two years, I sensed we were very much the same. But I could take that one step back. Most of them would never be given a similar chance.

I went into the precinct house and collected my last check. Goodbyes. All around me were goodbyes. Then I walked back into the street and the sun and the sound of people. When I got into my car, I paused for a moment. And then I thought of that child who smiled so readily, who sought the same sun and heard the same voices, and then I felt the wetness on my cheek. For a moment, I sat and listened to the street, knowing I would always hear it, and then I turned on the ignition and drove away.

From the most violent precinct in the city, I had been sent to one of the safest. My wife, Mary, appreciated it more than I did.

Most cops who work in high hazard precincts or units pay a high psychological price for such duty. Because of the requirement to be mentally alert at all times while on duty, it may take hours after a tour to reach homeostasis. Once that equilibrium with one's environment is secured, you're just a regular guy or gal again. However, over an extended period of such exposure, combat fatigue sets in and you're always ready for a fight.

Eventually, the department realized the detrimental effect of this process and started a rotation plan to counter the problem.

As a newly promoted captain, I entered a new world; a world of internal politics, coalitions and intrigue. All promotions above captain in the Police Department are made solely at the discretion of the Police Commissioner. There are no written tests to pass as with the ranks of sergeant, lieutenant, and captain. The test for those higher ranks are subjective ones. Only time can teach one how to swim in those waters. Hopefully, one will not drown while learning.

The C.O. of the 50th Precinct was Jack Bonner, a short man with a Napoleonic complex. As a new captain, I vowed myself to silence in hope of learning all the prevailing currents. Jack had a direct line to the commissioner and didn't hesitate to use it if someone got in his way. My democratic style of leadership was constantly scraping against his authoritative approach. His promotion and transfer were welcomed.

Headquarters selected a captain name Tim O'Shea as the new C.O. Tim was a tall, slim, handsome Irishman whose style contrasted dramatically with that of Bonner. Tim was calm and controlled under the worst conditions. He would listen quietly, absorb what was said, and then extract what was practical. He was a joy to work with – a real professional.

In the relaxed and verdant reaches of the Northwest Bronx, my mind shifted to more creative pursuits – I started to write jokes. When P.O. Mario Caturo, a Bronx borough aide, would call to give me my Duty Captain assignments (cover the borough at night, respond to shootings etc, investigate and write a report), I would try my jokes out on him. Some were actually funny. All were about borough bosses. Mario, who like me, enjoyed throwing gentle barbs, invited me to do a short routine at the Bronx borough Christmas/promotion party.

Then, another writing proposal gained currency in my consciousness. I figured that if Dennis Smith could write a book, "Engine Company 82", about firemen in the South Bronx, why couldn't I write a book about the cops at Fort Apache. And so began another journey down an uncharted and bumpy road.

Ray Mc Dermott was the Bronx Borough Commander. An Irishman with a thick, hard to understand brogue, he was tough, straight-forward, knew the streets and was a good boss to work for – the troops loved him.

However, shortly after Tim O'Shea came to the 50th Precinct, McDermott was replaced by Tony Bouza. McDermott was on the "old" team. Police Commissioner Cawley was conducting a purge of senior, conservative commanders in favor of younger, more progressive types.

Tony Bouza, born in Spain, was over 6 feet 4 inches tall, slim and had strong features. He came to the Bronx with a tough reputation; he detested incompetence. Groomed in the Planning and Inspections Divisions, he was known to carry an ever-ready and sharp hatchet.

There was a full house at that year's promotion party held at Steve's Castle Harbor restaurant. Steve served the best pork and sauerkraut you ever tasted. I hoped that my roast would be as well done. Among the more than 200 cops and bosses present were Sidney Cooper (of Serpico fame), Bouza and McDermott.

Mario Caturo introduced me, "Captain Walker would like to say a few words." I had each joke written out on a separate piece of paper, arranged in the hope that my first joke was the best. I fixed the mike. There was a buzz in the room (not for me – people just kept talking). A little acting was called for. I raised my voice and commanded, "Would you please lower the volume. I have an important announcement to make." I had their attention.

"The first thing I'd like to do tonight is to clear up an issue that has caused some consternation here in the Bronx. There's been a lot of speculation that the only reason Chief Bouza has replaced Chief McDermott is that Bouza speaks Spanish. That is just not true. The real reason is that McDermott doesn't speak English." There was a tremendous roar of laughter. If I could read lips, I think McDermott was saying, "You Son of a Bitch." And then he burst out into laughter.

I crumpled up the paper and threw it into the audience. An old Italian cop picked it up. This caused another outburst. We all figured he might be collecting evidence against me. Bouza was chuckling. I yelled to him, "Hey Tony, I love those little cotton balls on strings hanging from the rear window of your car" (a prevalent decoration in the South Bronx) – more laughter and so it went. I'd crumple the joke, throw it and the old cop would pick it up. Later, he facetiously told me, "I'm an ex-plainclothesman, never let Sidney Cooper get your handwriting sample." I smiled. Sidney was a feared "ubermenchen." And that's how I met my life-long friend, Lou Palumbo. Lou had somehow morphed from undercover cop into the Bronx borough messenger (He delivered the department mail to police headquarters and picked up all department mail for the Bronx).

Over the years, I learned a few things about doing these borough roasts:

One – There's a thin line between funny and mean. Keep it funny.

Two – All jokes must be about bosses.

Three – No matter how hard you try, some bosses are going to get pissed.

I decided to forget the jokes for a while and concentrated on writing about my adventures in Fort Apache.

Chief Bouza was busy too. It wasn't long before several precinct commanders felt the quick movements of Tony's hatchet and departed. Chief Bouza was a great believer in the axiom that a good staff makes a good C.O. He therefore gave precinct C.O.s an opportunity to get rid of their executive captains if they so desired. The only C.O. in the Bronx who took advantage of the offer was Brendan O'Sullivan, C.O. of the 43rd Precinct. Brendan's executive Captain was transferred and it was decided that I would replace him. I hated to leave Tim O'Shea and the men in the 5-0, but I wasn't consulted. I had a hunch that the reason was a bad joke.

A final goodbye was offered in the 50th Pct. newsletter. In addition, the 3rd paragraph outlined what I considered my major accomplishment as the 5-0's executive captain.

50th PRECINCT NEWSLETTER

No. 16   DATE: July 11,
1973
A FOND FARWELL: To Captain THOMAS WALKER, who will long be remembered by the many friends he made in the 50th ...... and a cordial welcome to our new Exec. Captain THOMAS HEFFERMAN, we hope his stay with us is rewarding.

COMMENDATORY LETTERS: A letter for P.O SCANLON and FENNY, for showing sympathy and understanding while handling a D.O.A......for P.O. GRENITO for being courteous when helping the public...for P.O. POUST and NAPOLITANO, for their handling of lost children case..... for LEMOLE and SPAROCINO for their handling of the accident case.....and for SGT. PIAZZA and P.O. HANNIGAN from the P.T.A. for the continued attention during the school year. And finally, to LT Gregor for sticking up for the late tour crew- no D.O.A.'s for them.

THE 50 SOFTBALL TEAM: Won their first (and hopefully not last) game of the season last week, beating the 34th Pct. 9 to 8. In the first inning P.O. PFEIFFER hit a tremendous homerun driving in two runs. The 34 battled back and finally took and 8 to 5 lead, but P.O. SAYRE who was tired of being the losing pitcher hit a three run homer and tied the score.

The 34 was still confident of victory until the 50 coach put in our secret weapon, CAPTAIN THOMAS (FLASH) WALKER. The captain came up with two out in the ninth and the 34 pitcher promptly walked "Flash." P.O. Smaller hit a ground ball that went through for a single, and the captain was off and running. To the surprise of everyone the captain didn't stop at second, nor did he stop at third, and he rounded the bag and headed home. The 34 shortstop realizing what was happening threw the ball home as "Flash" headed down the line. The 34 catcher fearing a line of duty death, promptly let a perfect throw go through his legs as the captain scored the winning run.

I was moving one step closer to the Four-one Precinct. The Bronx had 3 divisions, the 7th, 8th and 9th, each with its own radio frequency. I was moving back from the 9th Division to the 8th Division which covered the 41st, 43rd and 45th Precincts.

CHAPTER 2

▼

Brendan O'Sullivan was on the ropes in the 43rd Precinct. His crime statistics, although improving, were poor. Brendan was schooled in Ireland and still spoke with a brogue. He had spent many years in Internal Affairs fighting corruption before it became a popular thing to do. A fighter by nature, Brendan had once told me, "I always go for the jugular." A crafty politician himself, he quickly made friends of the politicians in the area. The most prominent being John Calandra, the local State Senator.

The biggest problem in the precinct was the robberies in Parkchester, a huge housing complex owned and operated by the Metropolitan Life Insurance Company. My mother, Kathryn, lived there at the time, right across from the precinct on McGraw Avenue. You can imagine my dismay when she was hit in the face multiple times and robbed in her building lobby by some punk. My father would turn over in his grave if I didn't catch the bastard.

I immediately instituted vertical building patrols, using my anti-crime team in all buildings, but concentrating on perimeter locations. Parkchester had a competent security force, but the perimeter buildings were especially vulnerable because they provided quick escape routes.

A month later, my anti-crime team arrested a 25 year old male for another robbery. It was my guy. It ameliorated my anger, but better than most, I knew the true cost. It didn't heal my mother's facial wounds or lessen her newly developed fear of crime, but it did satisfy her sense of justice. Sadly, that would have to be enough.

Although O'Sullivan constantly promoted anti-corruption practices, the precinct hadn't made a bribery collar in over 4 years (In fairness, he'd been the C.O. for only five months).

I decided to make an offer to the troops that they couldn't refuse. So, I announced at several roll calls that anyone making a bribery collar would not only get a day off, but would also be entitled to a weekend at O'Sullivan's Long Beach cottage.

It didn't take long. P.O. Cole brought in an 80 year old Italian man who offered him 50 dollars to overlook the running of a red light and his driving without a license. We all cringed. The gentleman told us, in broken English, that he had been driving in the Bronx without a license for 50 years and that this was the first time he had been stopped. I told Officer Cole to request that a family member respond to the precinct A.S.A.P. and that he should expedite the man's arrest procedure. I felt more than a little guilty, and like most acquired guilt, I wanted the source summarily removed. P.O. Cole wasn't happy either – he took some unmerciful kidding from his buddies. His response – he accepted the day off, but declined the weekend at the shore.

In spite of all the political intrigue that was going on in the 43rd Precinct, it wasn't lost on the borough command that a nasty and bloody war was going on the South Bronx, which included the lower sectors of the 4-3. I knew better than most what was happening because I was catching an unusual number of Duty Captain assignments. Mario Caturo assured me that he was only the messenger, but that certain parties wanted me to pull extra duties. I wondered if their intent was to keep me from helping O'Sullivan stabilize the 4-3 Precinct, which would soon be designated as a high hazard precinct. What does that mean? It means, "Hey guys and gals, don't forget to wear your bulletproof vests." (The problem was we didn't have vests at that time).

On September 17, 1973, I decided to stop at the Four-one after my 9 to 5 tour to say hello to Moe DeVito. I was jolted to discover that a major assault was being launched against the Black Liberation Army (BLA) at 1803 Bryant Avenue, a block away from where actress Ellen Barkin had grown up.

The Duty Captain, Terry Cosgrove was behind the desk. "Hey

Walker," he moaned, "If something is going down, it's either you or me catching the duty."

"It's a short, very special list we're on Terry"

Terry handed me a portable radio attuned to the assault team's frequency. We sat at the muster room desk monitoring that radio and the 8th Division radio frequency. I didn't know it then, but I would later be designated to write the required Interim Order 118 report to the Firearms Discharge Board evaluating the assault team's performance.

The BLA was an offshoot of the Black Panther party, the Cleaver faction. They didn't provide us with a copy of their roster, but we figured there were approximately 30 hardcore members, 35 associates and maybe a cadre of 50 sympathizers. They operated in cells of 3 to 5 members. Some cells traveled city to city robbing banks and attacking police officers. In a sense, they were left wing (Communist influenced) guerillas, who were in sympathy with the revolution going on in the 3rd world.

On November 29, 1972, the BLA assassinated P.O. Rocco Laurie and P.O. Gregory Foster in the 9th Precinct (other officers who died in the line of duty that year were Det. William Capers, P.O. Joseph Meaders, P.O. Elijah Stroud and P.O. Phillip Cardillo-murdered in a Harlem mosque.)

On February 9, 1973, a four man BLA team robbed a bank at 505 Southern Blvd in the Four-one Precinct.

Deputy Chief Harold Schryver, leading the 35 member assault team, assigned P.O. Michael Mortak of the 41st Precinct and his 8th Division portable radio to maintain liaison with the Communications Bureau (CB) and the Four-one Precinct. Mortak's partner, Robert Eugenia, on another frequency, relayed messages from Chief Schryver to the back-up team, Emergency Service Squad #3, parked on the corner of 174th Street and Bryant Avenue.

The target that evening was Robert Hayes, a known BLA member wanted for the June 5, 1973 murder of Transit Officer Sidney Thompson and the machine gunning of P.O. Pollina and P.O. O'Reilly in the 103rd Precinct.

Sidney, a 36 year old black officer with six years on the job, was attempting to arrest a fare beater at a Bronx subway station. While so engaged, an associate of the fare beater shot the officer. Despite being mortally wounded, Sidney was able to return fire and wound the shooter. Sidney was the 4th transit officer shot and killed since 1967 (Lloyd Innes, 1967; Michael Melchina, 1970; John Skagen, 1972). Sidney left behind a wife, son and daughter.

I noted at that time, as I stood there in the Four-one Precinct, that the BLA seemed to target teams of black and white officers. I prayed that no cops would be killed tonight.

Information was developed that the suspect, Hayes, lived in a ground floor apartment B-C at 1803 Bryant Avenue, a multiple dwelling. It was established that apartment B-C had been 2 separate 3 room apartments, but that a hole had been opened between the living room of apartment C into the kitchen of apartment B. The B and C apartments were at right angles to each other. If someone knocked at either door, the door in the other apartment provided, if so desired, a clear shot at the person knocking.

Chief Schryver's plan was to hit both doors simultaneously to eliminate that possibility. It also provided the strategic advantage of dividing the forces within the apartment. He also had officers stationed in the side alley, the rear alley, and court yard to prevent any window escapes. D.I. Gleason and Lt. Drum were to coordinate all the activity in the building itself.

We heard the order to close Bryant Avenue between 173rd street and 174th street. That news increased the cluster of officers crowding the desk. Then came a report that a large hostile crowd was forming behind the 174th Street barriers. The tension was palpable. It reminded me of being glued to the radio as a kid, listening to the Shadow or the Lone Ranger. But this was real. Then we heard it, "Officer down". "Those dirty bastards", I muttered. There were profanities all around me. "What the hell's going on", the radio squawked.

"All units stay off the air", C.B. ordered. Then C.B. quickly added," I need a 4-8 unit to respond to Vyse Avenue and the Cross Bronx Expressway." As I write this I remember staring out of the 13th floor kitchen window in the Nurse's Residence at Jacobi Hospital on 9-11 watching the second tower of the W.T.C collapse and stomping through the clinic screaming those same words, "Those dirty bastards, those dirty bastards."

Later, I would put together the required report on this raid. In so doing, I interviewed Sergeant Robert O'Neill and many others. It was obligatory that I interview any officer who had fired his weapon. In addition, I read all the reports they had submitted including those requesting departmental recognition. The essence of my report was as follows:

"On a prearranged signal both groups announced their identity and intentions and applied the ram to the individual door. Apartment door "B" failed to open. Lt. McBride and his group fell back from door "B'. Apartment Door "C" sprang open and Sgt. O'Neil, Det. Hardwick, Wright, Brown and Hay stormed into the apartment. Det. Wright saw a man (later identified as Robert Hayes) raising a shotgun, and shouted, "Gun." Hayes opened fire, striking Det. Betty. Detective Bobby Hardwick was also hit, taking a bullet to the left forearm. Det. Hardwick, seeing the seriousness of Betty's wounds, removed Betty to the hallway and then returned to the action. With each shot, the huge crowd at 174th St cursed and baited the Four-one Precinct cops who were securing the area.

In the hallway Lt. McBride administered first aid by applying a tourniquet to Betty's left arm, a handkerchief to his left hand. Due to the seriousness of the injury it was determined that Betty needed immediate medical attention. Betty was passed out of a rear window to the rear yard, helped to an adjoining street (Vyse Ave.) and escorted several blocks to the Cross Bronx Expressway. A 4-8 R.M.P. rushed him to Jacobi Hospital. Betty was admitted and remained there for 36 days.

Det's Wright and Brown exchanged fire with Hayes. Hayes repeatedly stuck his shotgun out of the bedroom doorway and fired. Det. Wright attempted to grab the gun's barrel, but Hayes would pull the gun back into the room. After several of these maneuvers, both Det's Wright and Brown stuck their guns around the wall, through the open doorway and fired into the room in an effort to neutralize the firing within, at which time Hayes surrendered with his wife and newly born child.

Upon entering the hallway of apartment "B" Sgt. O'Neil and Det. Jimenez advanced toward an unlit area of the apartment and were met by gunfire from Melvin Kearney and Avon White. Det. Jimenez was hit once in the left side by automatic gunfire and fell to the floor. Avon White continued firing at Det. Jimenez on the floor. Sgt. O'Neil returned the gunfire and pulled Det. Jimenez back into the kitchen out of the range of gunfire.

"One of the shooters inside the bed room set off a smoke bomb, but it failed to deter the detectives. The shooters shouted that they were surrendering and were coming out. Michelle Scott and Eleanor Brown came out first, followed by Melvin Kearney and Avon White. The prisoners were handcuffed and led out to the hallway, where personnel arranged for their escort to the 41st Pct. Det. Jimenez was removed by R.M.P. to Jacobi Hospital. He was admitted for gunshot wounds of the left side in the area of his waist. The bullet that struck Jimenez had passed through his body."

Despite 3 cops being wounded, the killers were removed and processed without getting so much as a scratch.

My I.O. 118 findings were as follows:

Even in a department deeply steeped in gallantry and heroics, the bravery and humanity of these fine officers will long stand as a source of inspiration and pride for us in this service and the public we serve. These officers deserve the highest award possible. Their actions, after announcing themselves and their purpose and being fired upon were well within the guidelines established by I.O. 118.

That was one battle won, but we had paid heavily for it. I returned to a different kind of war in the 43rd – a bureaucratic one.

In September '73, Bouza began his blitzkrieg against O'Sullivan. Bouza gave O'Sullivan a poor evaluation for the previous quarter. The Division Commander, Fandel, told Bouza that "O'Sullivan was trying his best and that Walker had been a tremendous help." During the interview Fandel also said O'Sullivan was "aggressive", would "use any means to project himself and his status", that he "wouldn't turn my back on him" and that he often wonders, "What is he up to next?"

Ed Haggarty of the P.B.A. had complaints about two disciplinary cases in the 4-3. Bouza interviewed me on 9/27/73. He would later claim that my interview convinced him that O'Sullivan wasn't a "very effective executive". My recollection was substantially different. The next day, September 28, 1973, Bouza advised the Chief of Field Services that he wanted O'Sullivan removed from his command and transferred out of the Bronx. Oh, it should be that easy.

As soon as the order to transfer O'Sullivan hit the wire, the

Leprechaun struck. With the help of State Senator John Calandra, he obtained a "Show Cause" order in Supreme Court from Judge Brust, who issued a temporary injunction against the transfer.

Police Commission Donald Cawley and his chiefs were outraged. It was the first time in the history of the department that such an action had been taken by the Commanding Officer of a precinct. The wheels of the borough ground to a halt. The Captain's Union loved it — Bouza wasn't one of their favorite chiefs.

For the next 5 weeks there was nothing but turmoil in the precinct. The local newspapers, the citizens groups, the local politicians all decried the attempted removal of O'Sullivan. The people simply loved the Leprechaun.

O'Sullivan and I were in his office when the Captain's Union delegate, Marty Wilson, stormed in waving the local paper. "We get Bouza by the nuts. We got him this time. The community is on your side Brendan".

O'Sullivan, an I.A.D. mentality to the end, asked me to "give them a second." I nodded, walked out and went to the muster room desk.

A few minute later, the cop on precinct security duty quickly entered the station house, knocked on the captain's door and announced, "Bouza's here!"

Marty Wilson came running out of O'Sullivan's office screaming, "Where's the rear exit, where's the rear exit?" I smiled, saying to myself, "Yeah, we have him by the nuts."

The "Show Cause" trial started shortly after that. Bouza was one of the first called. Apparently, he didn't handle Calandra's direct examination very well— his answers on how to stop apartment building robberies were particularly vacuous. He admitted doing poorly.

The chief called me at the precinct a few days after he testified. During our talk he mentioned that I was nearly ready for a Command, maybe in about 6 months. At no time during that conversation was my upcoming testimony discussed. I mention that because of what happened several days later.

Chief Reid, Bouza's second in command came to see me. Somehow he had learned of Bouza's suggestion that I might be ready for a command in 6 months.

Reid suggested that I should report the offer to I.A.D.., that Bouza was trying to influence my testimony. I told Reid that I didn't consider it a bribe offer, but if the question was raised at the hearing, I would answer the question truthfully.

"Wow", I told myself, "and this is the guy Bouza assigned to document the entire case. That's back-stabbing at its lowest".

Brendan O'Sullivan was always friendly, smiled a lot and spouted large chunks of blarney to me. I enjoyed the guy. It was easy to see why the community adorned him. But there was this other side of the man that he didn't share with me, but I knew it was there. Brendan was a captive of that secret world, the world of Internal Affairs, the world of spies. A world that says that nothing is how it appears. Where most saw a minor violation of department rules demanding a mild rebuke, he saw hidden corruption demanding strong decisive action i.e. splitting up partners and changing their squads.

The department had created a disciplinary monster and now they were out to destroy him. And I was one of their weapons.

But, the past was haunting me. My father had been abandoned by those having relevant evidence during his insubordination case years before. The officers with information favorable to my father feared retaliation from the Inspector involved. My book, "Death of the Bronx Cop", details the "organizational kill" of my father. I was a rookie at the time, but I swore to myself that I would never allow that to happen to me; to be afraid to tell the whole truth, as I saw it. I owed O'Sullivan nothing; I owed Bouza nothing; but I did owe my father.

Having been subpoenaed by the petitioner, Brendan O'Sullivan, I took the stand in Bronx Special Terms Part I, Judge Brust presiding.

DIRECT EXAMINATION
BY MR. CALANDRA:

Q Captain Walker, what is your present assignment?

A I am the executive officer in the 43rd Precinct.

Q Now, did there come a time when you had a conversation with Assistant Chief Inspector Anthony Bouza relative to Captain O'Sullivan?

A That is correct, yes.

Q And about when was that in point of months?

A. It was in September, approximately around the 25th

Q Would you tell us what was said at this meeting between you and Chief Inspector Bouza as to what you said and what he said as it relates to Captain O'Sullivan?

A Well, the chief was interested in finding out- - I don't want to set a background. The chief wanted to know, in light of recent events, how the capacity of Captain O'Sullivan to run his command was.

THE COURT: How long had you been there?

THE WITNESS: At the time of the conversation, about three months.

BY MR. CALANDRA:

Q Now, you indicate in light of recent developments that this conversation took place?

A I guess it would have to be Patrolman Garafolo and Miele.

Q How about Patrolman Hamptman or Fitzsimmons, did that come up?

A That wasn't an immediate problem, as I could see it. The immediate problem was Police Officer Garafolo and Police Officer Miele.

Q Now, with regard to this immediate problem of Miele and Garofolo, what was this conversation between you and Bouza about regarding this incident?

A Well, in light of that, the chief came in and he wanted to know, how is Brendan doing, is he upset, is he having any - - here again I am not using the chief's exact words. I'm trying to give you the general impression of what he said. He wanted to know, basically, the psychological mood of Captain O'Sullivan.

Q What did you say?

A I laughed and I said, "No, no, he is fine, there is no problem as I could see in that particular area."

Q Yes?

A And then from there he wanted to ascertain basically if Captain O'Sullivan should remain as the commanding officer of the 43rd Precinct.

Q   He asked your opinion on this question?

A   That's correct.

Q   What was your opinion?

A   My opinion was that at the present time Captain O'Sullivan should remain as the C.O. of the 43rd Precinct based on the fact that our productivity had increased, and we were moving in the right direction, that we had a good team going, and at this particular point in time, I felt that Captain O'Sullivan should continue as the C.O.

Q   You indicated a moment ago that the productivity increased; is that correct?

A   That is correct, yes.

Q   In these areas of crime, grand larceny-auto, burglaries, robberies, briberies, and so forth, am I correct these are all the categories you are talking about?

THE COURT: He didn't say bribery.

Q   Is bribery included with the category of crime?

A   Well, you could include it in the area- - it is a crime to try to bribe a police officer.

THE COURT: You say he was good in the area of corruption?

THE WITNESS: In the area of corruption and the area of community relations Captain O'Sullivan was outstanding. We did have an area as far as productivity was concerned and when I first came to the command it was my opinion that the command wasn't as production oriented as it should have been.

THE COURT: Is that -- is productivity always dependent on the captain of the precinct?

THE WITNESS: I guess it is like managing a ball club, if the ball club wins, the manager gets credit for it. If the ball club doesn't win the manager has to take the heat. So there are a lot of extenuating circumstances. But it is a tough position to be a C.O. of a precinct. There are a lot of things going on and it's not an easy job, it is a very challenging job. And I felt Captain O'Sullivan was doing a good job, but all managers are weak in certain areas, and whether it be productivity or community relations, it is incumbent upon the C.O. to build up a staff to compensate for his weaknesses. This is my own view on the situation.

THE COURT: Go ahead.

BY MR. CALANDRA:

Q Now, to get back to the question, on the question of production, does the factor of personnel have a bearing?

A (No response.)

Q Yes or no?

THE COURT: If you can't answer the question yes or no, answer it in any other way.

A It would have a bearing. It is a factor that should be included.

Q Now, Captain, isn't it a fact that when the captain became commanding officer and during the time he was commanding officer and during the time he was commanding officer, there was a reduction in personnel to the sum of 16 percent in the 43rd Precinct?

A I won't argue with the figures because I am not - -

I know there was a reduction in manpower, the exact figure   I couldn't give you.

Q Now, also, Captain, isn't it a fact that the 43rd Precinct has the largest population of all the precincts in New York City?

A We have a very large population. Whether it is the greatest in the city, there again I am not sure.

Q Now, you indicated this was your belief when you first came there, that maybe he wasn't too productive oriented. Was that also your belief in September?

A No, in my conversation with the chief I think indicated that we were moving in the right direction.

Q Isn't it a fact, Captain, that in all of the statistical areas that you people consider in the area of crime, such as bribery arrests, grand larceny-auto, right up the line, that there was a dramatic increase in percentage?

A   Well, we had a dramatic increase in G.L.A., in burglary, and very dramatic in bribery. Our productivity in the traffic area was excellent.

Q   How about intox driving?

A   Intox driving was good also, although it was not as drastic as you might suggest, and the only area where we were having a problem was the area of robberies.

Q   Now, in the area of robberies, when we talk about robberies do we only talk about robberies that are committed out on the street, or do we lump into that figure robberies that are committed on personal property, private property, such as vestibules?

A   Yes.

Q   Is there any indication in your statistical facts as to robbery, how many of these robberies as inside or outside, so to speak?

A   Yeah, we make a statistical breakdown on where the robberies occur, in what sectors, inside, outside, et cetera.

Q   And are part of these robberies the familiar so- - called purse-snatching type robberies?

A   Some purse snatchings are robberies and some are not. It depends on whether force is used. If a pocketbook is just snatched from the lady, and the youth or whoever it might be, flees the scene that would probably be classified as a grand larceny. If the woman holds on to her pocketbook and then she is belted a couple of times, this would be classified as a robbery.

Q   When you say that in the area of robberies it wasn't up or didn't move up as forward as much as you would like –

A   Right.

Q   Did you take into consideration the outside robbery when you take that in consideration, or do you lump all the robberies together, in and out?

A   All together.

Q   Is there any conceivable way a commanding officer can effectively decrease the number of robberies that occur inside, which is on personal, private property?

A   Well, certainly.

Q   How?

A   There are.

Q   How?

A   You have vertical patrols in the Parkchester area. We basically have a vertical command in the 43rd – I should say horizontal, I am sorry. We have a few projects, and then of course, we have Parkchester. In the area of Parkchester we conducted vertical sweeps which would enhance coming across a mugger or a rapist or a robber in the lobby.

Q   Was that being done?

A   Vertical sweeps, yes, to my knowledge, vertical sweeps were taking place. There is a lot that can be done; you can set up citizen patrols in lobbies. In fact, in the 43rd we are putting in reactors, volunteers to come in Parkchester to help us police that particular area. There are steps that can be taken in this particular area.

Q   And so, some of these steps were taken, were they not?

A   Yes, that is correct, yes.

Q   Now, one further question, this hearing started on October 5th in this same courthouse?

A   Yes.

Q   Did you receive a visit from Chief Inspector Bouza on October 9th, 4:15 p.m., at the precinct house?

A   I was spoken to by Chief Bouza numerous times since October 5th. He is my superior officer.

Q   I realize that.

A   So –

Q   The answer is yes?

A   I can't say yes - - I don't know. If somebody said they saw me talking to Chief Bouza at 4 o'clock on October 9th, I wouldn't disagree with them because there is a likelihood I might have been.

Q   In any of your visits - - in any of his visits

Q   Did you ever make the statement to Chief Bouza regarding O'Sullivan, and I quote, "O'Sullivan was not merely concerned with production"?

A   Well, here again I made a statement somewhat to that effect.

THE COURT: You mean to the chief inspector?

THE WITNESS: But not in that context.

To Chief Bouza, right. I said that when I first came to the command I felt that there was certain deficiencies and that I didn't feel at this particular point in time, when I first came in July of 1973, that Captain O'Sullivan was production oriented.

Q   But in the September meeting you felt at that point he had - -

A   I just - -

Q   I am sorry.

A   As far as production-oriented, I was talking in certain categories.

Q   Like what?

A   Well, let me just say this, there are three areas here again, I'm giving my own opinion. I always consider three areas very important: crime, community relations and corruption. Captain O'Sullivan was outstanding in the area of community relations and corruption. And I felt that the one area where he wasn't as strong was in the area of productivity. Like I say - -

Q   Well, let me - -

A   (Cont'g.) This was an evaluation I made when I first came to the command.

THE COURT: With reference to crime?

THE WITNESS: That is correct.

THE COURT: What did you mean by that, sufficient arrests?

THE WITNESS: I meant at the time we were getting a certain number of G.L.A. complaints a month and we weren't getting enough arrests in comparison to the complaints. Same thing applied in several other categories. But that was initially when I was assigned to the command.

BY MR. CALANDRA:

Q Yes, that was initially when you were assigned to the command - -

THE COURT: When you said "G.L.A.", it meant grand larcenies?

THE WITNESS: Right, grand larceny-auto.

Q That was your opinion in July?

A Yes.

In conversations with Bouza after October 5, did he ever discuss his testimony in court or what your testimony may be in court?

A No.

Q Never referred to this case at all?

A He told me, "Don't worry about it, Tom, it will all work out."

Q That is all he said about this case?

A Right.

Q Was that on September 27th, the day before he got his transfer?

A It might have been, might have been.

THE COURT: Any questions?

MR. WOLF: No cross-examination, Your Honor.

I didn't have long to wait for Bouza's evaluation of my testimony. Deputy Inspector Warren Knecht delivered the verdict later that day.

"You're dead, Tom", he offered gently. "Tony said you didn't bite the bullet." Knecht was a good guy. I kiddingly asked him, "So maybe, I'm not ready for a Command?" He laughed, then replied, "Well, not in the Bronx, that's for sure."

A few days later, the verdict was announced. O'Sullivan was out. The Court recognized that Police Commissioner's right to run his department, and D.I. O'Connell was the new C.O. of the 43rd Precinct. As for me, I was waiting for the other shoe to drop. It wouldn't take long. That "shoe" would take the form of a guy named Walter.

CHAPTER 3

▼

As with most travails, it started simply. Police officer Ray Rodriguez, one of the 43rd Precinct's Community Relations specialists, and I were going to a community meeting in the Castle Hill project. I had lived there in the sixties, but decided to seek a calmer environment upstate after my 8 year old daughter was bitten on her breast by one of the neighborhood girls (I would move back to the Bronx in 1971). Mayor Beame wasn't going to promote any captain to a higher rank if he lived outside the city. I got suckered on that one.

Ray and I were greeted that night by a full crowd in the local Chinese Restaurant. Heated complaints about street crime were the only items on the menu that night. There was no Column B. However, there was one complaint that Ray and I could immediately investigate – a room, buttressed by a black steel door, located down an incline behind the very row of stores where we were meeting. We proceeded to the location and knocked on the steel door. There was no response. A young black woman informed us that a private taxi company, run by a guy named Walter, used the space for gambling.

Now, that not only rang a bell, it sounded an alarm. Not only did I know Walter, but I had moonlighted driving one of his cabs when I lived in the project (you can't be lazy when you already have 4 children (one more to add in Nyack) and you're going to college at night for a Master's Degree).

I knew what was required and I did it. I asked Ray to prepare and submit an Intelligence Report re: Suspected gambling activity at the identified site.

I took a deep breath and forgot about Walter. Why? Because the 4-3 Precinct was under attack. A funneling cloud of crime had crossed the Bronx River from Fort Apache and was chewing up the southeastern sector of the 4-3.

As noted earlier, we had broken the ice on bribery collars and special inducements were no longer needed. So it wasn't surprising when three of my anti-crime officers, Jimmy Byrne, Joe Modica and Ed Snow, brought in an arrest for bribery.

I was congratulating myself and the officers in the muster room when the Desk Officer shouted, "Hey Cap, you got a phone call." I lumbered to the front of the desk and grabbed the phone. "Captain Walker, Can I help you?" It's me, you got one of my guys", was the response. "Who's me?" I asked "It's me, Walter."

"Oh shit", I told myself. "Can't I get rid of this guy"? Walter was persistent. He wanted to know if he could make a deal for the release of his man. I was tempted to simply say, "No", but I had some reservations. If I said "No," wouldn't that in a sense be corruption on my part.

The Department was in the middle of the Nadjari Investigation, a special prosecutor appointed to investigate corruption in the Criminal Justice System. The police were his main target. Phones were being tapped, conversations were being recorded, and, as some claimed, Gestapo tactics were being employed by the Nadjari team.

Things were moving fast. I didn't have much time to decide. O.K! So, I told Walter to come in and we'd see what we could do. Then, I called the Internal Affairs Division (I.A.D.), told them what I had and requested that they dispatch a team forthwith to the precinct. I just hoped that they would arrive before Walter. They did! No street cop is a fan of I.A.D.. – there's enough bad guys out there trying to stab you in the back.

In any event, I was happy to see them, especially Bill Killeen, a straight-shooter. I.A.D.. wired up one of my cops. When Walter arrived, my only job was to direct him to a side office to discuss the matter with the arresting officer. That done, I retired to my office and waited.

Ten minutes later, I.A.D. and the arresting officer, bubbling over, returned with the tape. We played it. All agreed that Walter had offered a bribe to free his man. They then returned to the office to record the acceptance of the deal. That done, Walter was arrested. Walter wanted to talk to me. I instructed the officer to tell Walter that "it would be foolish of me to ever talk to him again."

It wasn't a pleasant experience for me. Sure, as a traffic cop, I'd let a guy off with a warning if he had his wife and kids in the car. But Walter should have known better. Not this! I shook my head and once again, forgot about Walter.

A few days later, I was notified that Assistant District Attorney (A.D.A.) Giovancetti in D.A. Merola's office wanted to see me.

When I entered the ADA's office, Giovancetti's feet were up on the desk, telephone in hand. Upon seeing me, he immediately hung-up the phone and pointed to a chair slightly off-center in front of his desk. I plopped down. He didn't move.

"You heard about the 18 minutes gap in the Nixon tapes?

"Absolutely", I replied

"Well, there's a 6 minute gap in Walter's tape

"Oh, no," was the best I could offer. Walter wasn't going away.

"I hear you have a B.S. in Physics from City College"

"Right, and a Masters in Public Administration"

"Interesting", he replied, nodding his head and blinking his eyes.

I got the message; it was time to defend myself. I calmly explained how the case developed and that I.A.D.. had complete control of the situation. I then filled him in on my prior association with the defendant.

Giovancetti hadn't moved, his eyes staring upward in thought, his feet still up on the desk.

"Would you go out into the hallway and ask Harry to come in?" he requested coolly.

"Are you finished with me? I asked

"No, I'm not," he forcibly stated. I didn't like his tone. "Excuse me," I said. "I'm a captain in the New York City Police Department, I'm not your fuckin' lackey. If you want Harry, get off your ass and get him yourself."

Giovancetti quickly removed his feet from the desk, pushed his chair backward and shouted "You can leave now."

I left. On the way out of the building, I met Detective Charlie Jenks. Charlie was not only a friend, but one of D.A. Merola's bodyguards.

"How did it go?", he inquired.

I told him. Charlie laughed saying, "I'm sure I'll see you here again." Charlie was wrong!

The next day I was directed to report to Nadjari's Special Prosecutor's office on the 57th floor of the World Trade Center.

I conferred with a colleague, Captain John Salo at the borough office. "Be careful, these guys are headhunters," he warned. "Get a lawyer."

Governor Nelson Rockefeller had accepted the recommendations of the Knapp Commission and named a super prosecutor, Maurice Nadjari, a tall, slender, taciturn, 48 year old former Hogan staffer for the job.

The new inquisitor for the job would have gargantuan powers, the likes of which New York had never experienced. All New York District Attorneys except Mario Merola in the Bronx were furious, especially the legendary Manhattan D.A. Frank Hogan.

When, at Christmas in 1972, Police Commissioner Murphy announced that hundreds of pounds of heroin and cocaine were missing from the police Property Clerk's office in Manhattan, D.A. Hogan immediately convened a Grand Jury. He was challenging Nadjari's exclusive power to investigate such matters. Nadjari's men, with Rockefeller's o.k., busted into the Grand Jury room and physically stopped the proceedings. Nadjari was king. However, as scandal after scandal rocked New York, the political pressure on the two hundred lawyers in Nadjari's office was tremendous – they needed bloodied bodies.

While Nadjari had the power to investigate all parts of the Criminal Justice System, and he did, the arrest and conviction of corrupt cops was his top priority – it's easier to catch a street cop than a crooked Judge.

It got so bad in the N.Y.P.D. that lunch rooms had to be established in every precinct – you couldn't be caught if you weren't out there.

In retrospect, I know I should have taken John Salo's advice and requested a union lawyer, but I told myself, "You haven't done anything wrong. Why do you need a lawyer?"

It was over a quarter of a century before September 11, 2001 when

I stepped into the elevator in the South Tower of the World Trade Center. I will never forget that ride. I was terrified. It was a cattle car. The elevator banged wildly from side to side as it lumbered upward. To say I wasn't impressed by the construction of that elevator would be an understatement. If the construction of those elevators was representative of the general construction of those towers, I'd have to conclude that the builder was guilty of malfeasance.

Not only does the Empire State building have great elevators, but on July 28, 1945, at 9:40 a.m. on a foggy morning, a B-25 crashed into the 79th floor of the Empire State Building killing thirteen people (mostly young girls working in the Catholic Relief office) and injuring 26 others. A scientist in the building at the time stated. "The building moved twice and then settled." Enough said!

Having survived the elevator ride to the 57th floor, I was ushered into Prosecutor Shine's office. Shine, young, thin and professional, welcomed me.

"Where's your lawyer?" he asked, looking toward the door.

"I didn't think I needed one "I replied." I didn't do anything wrong.

"Then, why are you're here?" He countered

"You really want to know?

"It's a good place to start."

For the next two hours, I explained the saga of Walter, the I.A.D. intervention, and the revenge of the Bronx D.A. Shine wasn't impressed.

Now, I'm the kind of person who likes to settle problems A.S.A.P. Apparently, Nadjari's people sensed that trait in me and decided to let me swing in the wind for the next two years before letting a Grand Jury decide my fate.

It wasn't long after that W.T.C. appearance that the other shoe dropped. In fact, it was only 13 days after Walter had been arrested that I heard I was being transferred again. I figured that I'd be heading out of the Bronx, but to my surprise, I was being sent back to the 41st Precinct.

Now, I'm not trying to make myself out to be some kind of a crusader. I know I wasn't always ultimately in the right, but when I look back on my actions I have no regrets. Sometimes I even manage a chuckle. But there was a price to pay. I accepted that.

It would have killed headquarters to know it, but I was happy to be sent back to Fort Apache. A lot of my friends were still there. Guys like Moe DeVito, Dave Cohen, and Murray Ellman, the best street cops I ever knew and so many others. We had gone through hell together. They send me back not knowing they were doing me a favor – a big favor.

CHAPTER 4

▼

Legend comes hard to the Bronx. Most of those legends that persisted came from Yankee Stadium where men performed by contract, by design. Other than that, the Bronx remained the forgotten borough of New York City. Unless there was a spectacular murder, or a large drug raid, news of the Bronx was lucky to make page 40 or be broadcast during the waning moments of the six o'clock news. When you thought of New York, you imagined Manhattan as its mansion, Staten Island and Queens as its lawns and Brooklyn as its scullery. The Bronx became the city's jakes.

Don't attach bitterness to this observation. The reason for the Bronx's condition was as much geographical as it was social. When the great post-war emigration from the city began, the Bronx became a junction for those moving north to Westchester and Connecticut, or west to Northern New Jersey. True, the well-to-do had established themselves in Riverdale, along the Hudson River, or moved up to Jerome Avenue and the Grand Concourse. But as the population of blacks and Puerto Ricans grew and moved across the Harlem River, those whites fleeing the central city leap-frogged the borough. Those that had settled there, the Irish and the Italians who had sought the Bronx's greenery after experiencing the ghettos themselves, moved again. It was natural for the newcomers to discover the Bronx. Most of the major subway lines follow a north-south axis. This made travel easy for those who lacked cars or needed inexpensive transportation. When rents were raised, families increased in size or buildings became uninhabitable, they boarded the uptown IRT and headed north.

That's when the legend began. The exit point for many of the blacks and Puerto Ricans from Manhattan's Upper East Side was the Willis Avenue Bridge, the Third Avenue Bridge and the 138th Street Bridge. Two IRT lines, The Jerome Avenue and the Pelham Bay lines snaked through the area. So the path these immigrants followed led to the South Bronx. And there they stuffed themselves into rotting tenements and learned on those cruel streets that the world offered them no more north of the river than it did south of the river.

As urban renewal eliminated many lower income people from Manhattan's West Side, the problem became aggravated. Many of them were pushed into that same area of the Bronx and they brought their problems and frustrations with them. A part of that section was designated by the police as the 41st Precinct; the Four-one.

Some newcomers brought conspicuous vices: prostitution; drug addiction; alcoholism, and nearly all forms of petty and violent crime. By the late 1960's, the four-one earned the dubious distinction of being the roughest precinct in the police department. It exceeded all other precincts in most of the classifications of serious crimes. A policeman assigned to the precinct quickly lost any sense of disbelief. It all happened in the four-one and you just had to cope with it. The precinct became a sort of outpost of civilization, as we understand the word. So the legend began.

In the late 60's Lt Lloyd Gittens christened the precinct, "Fort Apache." The incredible barbarity, the viciousness, the self-destructive vice far exceeded that found in more publicized areas of New York such as Harlem or Bedford Stuyvesant. In fact, the murder rate of this area exceeded such substantial cities as Kansas City and Miami. If ever an area of humanity had, however unconsciously, decided to let the Twentieth Century sweep by unnoticed, it was the four-one.

A great many slums in our major urban areas have been compared to hell, but all those areas possessed some redeeming factors. Vast areas of habitable housing still stood; the family structure remained intact; a sense of community preserved and there were always ways out and upward toward the stability of the middle class. None of these factors existed in the four-one. Life became less valuable than a subway token.

And on the streets filled with shards of glass and in the crumbling tenements, men and women fought daily for survival.

Into this horrible pit, the policeman stepped. In every instance, these were men subjected to awful forces that were beyond their control; and these were the men ostensibly hired to bring these very forces under control. Here were men, many of them the sons of immigrants, steeped in the belief that the city meant opportunity, and they themselves represented those very laws that regulated society and made possible such opportunity. Now this past and this authority, so deeply rooted in our middle class mythos was being contested, if not defied. These men tried to adjust, but as palpable symbols of that mythos they operated only as scouts or point men of a society that preferred to contain rather than solve its problems.

I never proposed nor do I know specific solutions to the problems of poverty. I can only depict some of its manifestations. Indeed, I would not assert that all the violence, all the hate in the four-one was a direct result of poverty. But what I can describe is the feeling I had for the men who served in the Four-one: their faithfulness to duty; their adherence to the law; their sincere efforts to aid the citizens of the Four-one. I can also tell of heroic efforts by some of those citizens to rise above their degrading surroundings. To me as a human being, the four-one was a distinct shock. I came, however, to regard the spirit of the men who worked there and those who lived and worked in the area as a distinct embodiment of man's ability to survive excruciating adversity. So it was that on St. Patrick's Day, March 17, 1974, I picked up my uniforms at the 43rd Precinct and prepared to return to Fort Apache. I tried to deduce the real reason Chief Bouza had opted to transfer me there, rather than, as most expected, out of the Bronx. I searched the past for answers.

Chief Bouza was well aware of the "Fort Apache Syndrome". As the head of the Inspections Division, he had interviewed Deputy Inspector William Burke Jr. after his removal from the 41st Precinct. Burke, a tough but likeable ex-marine described the syndrome as, "We're in the worst place on earth, we work harder than anyone else, no one cares about us, so therefore, we are entitled to do as we please because the normal rules don't apply to us."

Burke told Bouza that the reason he was dumped was because

Deputy Commissioner of Legal Matters Neco had badmouthed him to Ben Ward and Don Cawley re: his handling of Community Affairs. Chief Bouza quickly sent a report of the Burke interview to Wayne Kerstetter, a special assistant to the Police Commissioner.

In that report, Bouza said, "maybe they should plant some trees in front of the stationhouse".... "And even transferring the unfit to some inconvenient place." And "I believe people can be banished from the Four-one."

I know that many of the 400 cops who worked there would have loved to be banished to some inconvenient place.

Captain Marvin Boland replaced Burke as C.O. of the Four-one. Boland was highly intelligent, but he had the personality of a bureaucrat — mechanical.

In his April 26, 1972 Inspection report re: the 41st Precinct, Bouza was perplexed as to why the 8th Division commander had rated Boland number 2 instead of number 1 of 3 in the division. He wrote, "Is it possible that Inspector Connilie, a talented, intelligent, but orthodox commander is repelled by Captain Boland's iconoclasm."

Bouza was half right. Most of us were repelled by Boland, but it wasn't his iconoclasm, it was his personality. Maybe Inspector Connilie was more perceptive than Bouza realized. (I was promoted 4 months later in August of 72.)

As I was leaving the 43rd Precinct on that March 17th afternoon for the Four-one, I met Deputy Inspector Warren Knecht.

"Good luck, Tom," he offered, shaking hands. "You'll need it, I hear."

Obviously, Warren knew something I didn't. He was hesitant to enlighten me, but since he had alluded to a problem, he felt compelled to spill the beans.

It appeared that the real reason I was being sent to be in charge of investigations at Fort Apache was that the present captain in charge of the squad, Barney McRann, was being terrorized by his 2nd in command, Lt. Bill McHugh, and had requested an immediate transfer. It was hoped that the inevitable explosion between myself and the lieutenant would force both of us from the department. Warren said that the joke at the borough office was "Walker seemed to be able to handle the Leprechaun, let's see how he handles the Hulk."

I had expected to get a big hug from Carmen, the civilian precinct receptionist, as I entered the precinct, but she had, to my regret, retired. Bob Butler, our basketball star, greeted me with a flying hand slap.

In fact, new faces outnumber the old, but nevertheless, I received a warm welcome. I searched out Moe, Sergeant Saverin and Dave Cohen, my particular favorites, to fill me in on what I missed. I knew, after a 19 month absence, that a lot of funny, sad, and crazy things must have happened.

Sergeant Saverin told me about a private crematory that went out of business and deposited the canister remains of 80 clients into a vacant lot off Fox Street.

Moe told me that they hadn't found any more gorillas, but that a 20 foot shark turned up in the middle of an intersection on Southern Boulevard.

Dave told me that he had been challenged to a fist fight by some macho street fighter on Fox Street. It was arranged after one of Dave's 8 to 4 p.m. tours. There was a big turnout. Dave told me, "It was a good fight, the kid was tough, but I managed to get the best of him." George Pearson gave me a high five. Pearson and Big George Hankins were great guys. Off duty, they had opened the "Fort Apache Boxing Club" to help keep the community kids out of trouble. I was happy to see that Fran Jefferies, Diana, Beverly and the rest of the civilian clerical staff were still holding down the Fort.

It took a couple of days to settle in before I started to evaluate the changes that had taken place in the Four-one. Apparently Joe Sampson, the present C.O., had managed to create a healthy work environment which boosted the morale of the troops. During my absence, the department had accelerated a career path system which allowed officers with several years in busy shops to transfer to lighter houses. Some of the best cops had moved on (Andy Rosendzwerg and Tony Bimbo came to mind), but we still had a cadre of officers who just couldn't handle a place like the Four-one.

City services in the precinct had been improved. The Sanitation Department was doing an outstanding job cleaning the streets and removing trash. The Fire Department continued to do an impossible job in an admirable way.

I found that the precinct was being burned down little by little.

Some claimed that local elements were doing it to accumulate blocks of properties at low prices, properties which have great value due to their location. Regardless of who was doing it, the result eventually meant less work for the precinct. As the buildings burned, the people left. I estimated that 40,000 people had left the area since my departure in August of 1972. While our radio runs (calls for service) had decreased, our violent criminals had remained. Homicides, rapes, felonious assaults and robberies still plagued us. The men in the precinct remained the most shot at and assaulted group of policeman in the country.

From March 13, 1974 to March 23, 1974, 20 officers had been shot at with rifles, shotguns and pistols. On March 13, 1974, 8 armed men and one pistol packing Mama were in the process of holding-up a bar and grill when Ralph Freidman and his partner arrived on the scene, exchanged fire with the robbers, which caused the bandits to flee empty handed (2 were arrested later that day).

During this period of March Madness, Bob Coopman, apparently disliked because of his no-nonsense approach to crime on 174th street, was fired upon and returned fire two nights in a row. Bob asked for the next night off. It was granted.

On March 22, 1974, a man, later identified as a Black Panther, was exchanging gun fire with two uniformed officers on Interval Avenue. Anti-crime officer, Ralph Freidman, from the roof of a car, jumped the culprit and after a struggle was able to subdue, disarm and arrest him. (And so began the legend of "Superman.")

On the 23rd, we had another shooting and then the fever broke. March Madness had ended. The score — we won, only 3 officers injured. Once again, we would lead the city in shoot-outs that year.

Before I retired, Ralph Freidman would have been in 15 shoot-outs. Yes, 15 shoot-outs. But in seven (7) of those, as in the case of the Black Panther, Ralph never fired a shot, instead using his extraordinary physical abilities to help decide the issue. In those seven (7) shoot-outs, only his partners discharged their weapons.

In the eight (8) that Ralph returned fire (he always carried 2 weapons), he killed 3 shooters, wounded 2 and the other 3 either surrendered or escaped. In the Four-one Precinct, two of his favorite partners were Bob DeMatos and Edwin Fennell. I was generally the investigating officer preparing the I.O. 118 report on these shooting, so I was well aware of the dangers that all of our officers were constantly exposed too.

Shortly, after midnight, several months later, Ralph and Bob DeMatos (anti-crime officers wear civilian attire) were watching a group of kids panhandling on Fox Street. A man passing-by became agitated with the kid's tactics. They called him cheap. He simply pulled a gun out of his jacket, shot one of the 15 year olds in the chest, and fled down Fox Street. Ralph and Bob jumped out of their car, announced their status and ordered the man to freeze. The man stopped, turned and opened fire on the officers. Castro then jumped behind a car to reload. Ralph and Bob split up, moving car to car on opposite sides of Fox Street, hoping to secure two lines of fire on the shooter. The battle raged for 5 minutes before the shooter, hit multiple times, collapsed. He was D.O.A. Sadly, so was the 15 year old.

Ralph and Bob were awarded the Combat Cross, the 2nd highest award in the N.Y.P.D.

Ralph has been stabbed, bitten, suffered a fractured skull and has twice broken bones in his hands. He's made over 2,000 arrests, including 15 bribery collars. Super, indeed.

But while Ralph, Billy Rath and the rest of Sgt. Battaglia's crew were shooting it out with street thugs, I had another of my bureaucratic shoot-outs developing.

In street situations one has to make quick decisions. Some are easy — the guy is pointing a gun at you or charging at you with a knife.

But is ordinary encounters for me, the quickest and most effective evaluation I can make of an individual is by looking at his or her eyes— the mirrors of the soul.

Now, these evaluations, while necessary, are not always correct. But in the case of Detective Lieutenant Bill McHugh my evaluation was right on target—a bull's eye.

McHugh, a large muscular ex-boxer, had the eyes of a killer Bengal tiger on the hunt. I quickly decided that he was not a man to be trifled with—strictly professional would be my approach. However, I was 6 feet 3 and 300 pounds, so if and when it came to blows, it would be dandy of a fight. Even though I had an age and weight advantage, he had experience and something I didn't have—a winning record (I was 5 and 5 in my Army career).

I saw myself as a plump John Wayne and McHugh as Victor McLaughlin in "The Quiet Man." I sensed that everyone was waiting for the big event. I even envisioned Inspector Joe Sampson as Ward Bond, the priest and moderator in the film.

What did McHugh think of me? I don't think he liked me either. He rarely spoke off-the-cuff to me. I never saw him smile and he never came into my office, which was separated from his by a metal, floor to ceiling, wall divider.

As noted, my best course of action was to treat him strictly professionally. If I had something to tell him, I'd call him on the phone. Yes, it was that bad.

But in spite of all that, I had great respect for one action he had taken over a decade before we met.

There was a case in Lodi, New Jersey that had turned my stomach. In 1963, two uniformed Lodi police officers, Sergeant Peter Voto and P.O. Gary Tedesco responded to a disturbance at The Angel Lounge on Route 46 in Lodi. They were ambushed, forced to strip, humiliated and then shot to death by two sick bastards, Thomas Trantino and Frank Falco.

A massive search for the killers began. Falco was located hiding out in a rooming house in the 13th Precinct in Manhattan.

McHugh crashed into the room. Falco reached for his gun and McHugh shot the bastard dead. After that, Trantino quickly surrendered. After his trial, he was sentenced to death, but New Jersey repealed the death sentence and his sentence was commuted to life in prison.

In 2002, despite ferocious protests, Trantino was released from prison. Just another case of "Shame on New Jersey."

There are crimes that demand that earthly forgiveness never be sanctioned – this was one of them.

My clashes with McHugh had one positive effect – they helped me re-acclimate to the rhythms of the precinct. Things moved rapidly and violently down here. But thank God, I had a tough and gutsy detective squad. Guys like Bill Giblin, Bill Lally, Glen Johnson and so many others.

Giblin and Johnson had done a great job on the death threat against P.O. Ralph Squillante. If I recollect correctly, it was closed as an "exceptional clearance". They knew who had made the threat, had neutralized the danger, but they didn't have enough evidence to make an arrest (I saw Ralph last year – he's still the most happy fellow).

We had two detectives in the squad whom I called, "initial detectives". Even after 40 years, I hesitate to use their full names.

Det. B had been undercover in the Jewish Defense League – that story is yet to be told.

Det. R had been a bodyguard for Malcolm X. He and his wife were there the night Malcolm was assassinated in the Audubon Ballroom in Harlem. Det. R told me that during the assassination some coins were thrown onto the stage and that his wife, sitting in the first row, was so upset and confused that she crawled up onto the stage and started to pick-up the coins.

Of course, there's that famous photo of Det. R trying to save Malcolm's life by giving him mouth to mouth resuscitation on the ballroom stage.

Much like the Leprechaun, McHugh was having disciplinary problems with a few detectives. He was also treating Morris, the clerk who helped me prepare my I.O. 118 reports, disrespectfully. I never actually witnessed it, but I decided to challenge him on it anyway.

McHugh was in his office. I was in my office. I rang him on the phone. "Will you please stop being disrespectful to Morris, he doesn't appreciate it."

He didn't answer. Then, all of a sudden there was an explosion, something hit the wall dividing us. I was startled. I ran out of my office. Six detectives were moving toward McHugh's office. One yelled, "Oh, my God."

When I got to his office, McHugh was laying face down, his head up against the room divider. As I approached him, I could see what had happened. The bottom draw of his desk was open and as he got up, probably in an agitated state, he tripped over the draw, flew forward and hit his head on the wall– a T.K.O.

He was groaning. Several detectives helped him to his feet. He just needed some first aid.

If there was ever a chance of a reconciliation between us, that ended it. A week later, he applied for a "line of duty" injury. I turned it down citing "negligence" on his part. I had drawn a line in the sand.

I was in my office. McHugh was in his office. He called me out.

We faced off, 10 feet apart, guns holstered, in the squad office of Fort Apache. No, this was not "OK Corral," not even a cheap remake of "The Quiet Man." It was just a shouting match. Detective Jimmy Byrne, ready to referee, was disappointed. More words – and then it was over.

Word of the non-event spread quickly through the stationhouse. D.I. Sampson was well aware of all the problems on the 2nd floor. McHugh had a lot of issues. While I was no saint, apparently my positives, outweighed my negatives. McHugh retired shortly thereafter. With McHugh gone, D.I. Sampson moved me downstairs to be the Operations Captain.

CHAPTER 5

▼

When darkness fell, fires lit the night sky, a pyromaniac's delight; firemen swung hydrant wrenches to ward off crazed looters; the crack of gun shots echoed through fire-guttered buildings; sirens wailed as bullets filled bodies crumpled in hallways and on city sidewalks, only 87 murders last year — things were looking up; cops and detectives making arrests ducked as debris rained down from building tops; bodega owners loaded their shotguns or .22 caliber revolvers, this time they'd be ready; young women checked the gates on their fire escape windows, the nightstalker was still out there. And so it went, every night since my return, for the last six months.

The nightstalker, a dangerous psycho rapist, had been targeting young Hispanic women since the spring. The 23ish, male Hispanic was credited with 15 rapes and sodomies, but I figured he had greatly exceeded that number. My thinking was that many young women just wouldn't want to endure any additional trauma — police, neighbors, hospital, etc.

We had a good description (after 15 rapes I would hope so); an excellent M.O. (hits mostly around 3 a.m. on weekends, favors Sundays); Armed with a knife and gun. On two occasions he encountered the victims' husband at home and forced the husband to have intercourse with his wife. Then the nightstalker raped the wife.

The Hispanic media was rightfully outraged. We were doing our best, but this guy was slippery. Sooner or later, he was going to kill one of them.

We'd set-up surveillance teams in abandoned buildings every night from 11p.m. to 5 a.m. We doubled our coverage on weekends. We sit in burned-out apartments with various views of the streets — our binoculars and radios at the ready.

A guy comes out of a building – fits the description. We'd call in a car to pick him up. A guy coming down the street fits the description — this one we follow. Twice we thought we had him — wild chases, but he got away. Was it him? Or was it just a good citizen afraid of being mugged by these guys in civvies running after him? We had detectives and police officers working on their own time trying to catch this madman. Lt. Joe Bausano of the Bronx Sex Crime Squad assigned three detectives to help us, A. Cuesta, T. Kelly and H. Bellomo.

Everyone was helping. Duffy, Mahan (no relation to Kenny) and Bill Giblin from the squad. Murray Ellman, Neil Lorenz, Moe DeVito and Billy Rath were also most generous with their time. On the distaff side, I was informed that Robin Schwartz and Joann Catanese showed great zeal in this pursuit.

In the end, the victims deserved much of the credit for the capture of this monster. Given only a glance, what can a woman do that a man can't? Right, give a great description of what the person was wearing. Yes, and under torturous conditions, these victims managed exactly that. So it was that we knew that the nightstalker always wore brown, 2 tone shoes made of leather and suede. I thought that was astounding.

A second item that struck my interest was a teacher's aide who reported her Leggett Avenue attack two months after it happened. Why? Earlier that day, a neighbor had advised her that she had seen a man at the teacher aide's fire escape window the night before. Moe DeVito, now the Four-one Precinct's Intelligence Officer, told me, "Boy, was that woman frightened". I decided to give that lady special attention — I was certain that the nightstalker planned a return visit.

Two detectives working that area spotted a guy in an alley fitting the description. He appeared drunk. They noticed that he was wearing brown, 2 tone shoes made of leather and suede. They brought him into the stationhouse. A line-up was arranged and two of his victims identified the culprit. The guy was cold, never said a word, but the sun had risen on the nightstalker — a conviction followed.

I was still catching more than my share of duties. But, to be truthful, I enjoyed them — it was a break, a chance to eat at a nice diner without hearing gun shots or breaking up a fist fight.

It was a sight rarely seen in the 48th Precinct — a shiny new 1974 blue Mercedes with Pennsylvania plates cruising west down a cheerful, Christmas decorated Tremont Avenue at one-thirty in the morning. There was only one kind of Santa who drove a Mercedes and gave out candy down here and it wasn't the traditional one. This Santa dispensed candies known as heroin.

Police officer's Duffy and Von Werne, patrolling that area, spotted the car and its plates, looked wide-eyed at each other and just nodded.

The vehicle occupied by three black men was stopped. At that very moment, the 7th Division dispatcher broadcast an alarm for three male blacks wanted in connection with a robbery in the adjoining 46th Precinct. A back-up unit was requested and quickly arrived (P.O.'s Dumphy and Ohranberger).

P.O. Von Werne ordered the occupants out of the vehicle. As the men started to comply P.O. Dumphy observed the man in the back seat drop a 5 shot .38 caliber Smith and Wesson revolver to the floor. The three men were summarily arrested. The driver of the rented Mercedes asked, "Can't we work something out?"

The officer requested C.U. to give the Sergeant on Patrol a 10-85 at their location. After arriving, Sgt. Beattie spoke to the vehicle's driver and then suggested that they work this out at the stationhouse. A short time later, P.O. Lyons, working the borough wheel, called me at the Four-one Precinct.

"Cap, you got a gun and bribery collar in the 4-8."

"How much is a gun collar worth this year?

"How's 130,000 dollars sound?

"What?"

"Oh, yeah. The guy they arrested is Nicky Barnes."

"Not Leroy "Nicky" Barnes?"

"The same. Biggest heroin dealer in Harlem and the Bronx and points unknown."

"And a guy out on bail for homicide."

"The papers will be all over this one."

"I'm on my way"

In the trunk of the Mercedes were four grocery bags and a blue suitcase. The grocery bags contained 114, 319 dollars wrapped in 1000 dollar bundles bound with rubber bands. There was no bill larger that a 20. The blue suitcase held 18,675 dollars.

The precinct stationhouse was surprisingly subdued as I entered. Once situated in a side office, I conferred with Sgt. Beattie. He filled me in on the details of the arrest, that he had notified I.A.D., that they were responding, and that a search of the prisoners had uncovered another gun, but it wasn't on Nicky Barnes.

I immediately realized that the gun rap against Barnes was in jeopardy. The two guns recovered belonged to the other two men, not Barnes. If a gun was found on the floor of the car and you didn't see who dropped it, it could be attributed to everyone in the car.

But I had work to do. I first notified Public Affairs of the arrest — it was Christmas time and turning down a bribe of this magnitude was good publicity for the N.Y.P.D. I then called the Bronx D.A.'s office and conferred with Assistant District Attorney Gould.

The F.B.I. and the Intelligence Division were also notified. Captain Tim O'Shea, my former boss in the 5-0 Precinct, working the late tour in his own precinct, stopped by to see if I needed any assistance. He decided to stay.

I started to write my report. Tim got us some coffee. I called I.A.D. again. Things were dragging on. We needed a wire. Timed slipped by.

I.A.D. still hadn't arrived. Sgt Beattie was handling the negotiations with Nicky Barnes. They agreed on a deal — one of Barnes men would take the arrest for the guns, Barnes would keep the blue suitcase, and the officers could keep the rest. Once the transaction was complete, all three men were arrested for gun possession and bribery. Sgt. Beattie and his men had done a great job. It was in the D.A.'s hands now. However, as Yogi Berra once said, "It ain't over, till it's over."

It must have been around 3:15 a.m. The Bronx District Attorney, the Honorable Mario Merola stormed into the office with one of his bodyguards. He was pissed.

"You notified Public Affairs and you never notified us."

"Wait a minute," I replied. "I notified A.D.A. Gould right away. Right after I notified Public Affairs."

"Yeah, Public Affairs, " he noted sarcastically, "but not us."

"I spoke to A.D.A. Gould."

We parried for a few more minutes and then he said," This stinks, Captain."

"And so does being sent to Nadjari's office, Mr. D.A."

That remark infuriated the District Attorney. He turned and walked toward the door saying, "This isn't over Captain. You'll get yours."

"Give it your best shot," I yelled back. And then he was gone. I turned to Tim O'Shea and said "You didn't say anything."

"I thought you were handling it quite well," he replied, chuckling.

Mario Merola and I had several mutual friends — all said, he was a real decent guy. I knew that he was an outstanding District Attorney— not many D.A.'s concerned about a case, personally come out at 3 in the morning. We were both doing our best to serve, but sometimes life's script is so written that who plays the role of protagonist and who plays the role of antagonist is not clearly defined.

In the Bronx, Nicky Barnes was "Mr. Untouchable." He would beat the homicide, bribery and gun charges.

On January 19, 1978, he was sentenced to life imprisonment in Federal Court in Manhattan for drug trafficking. He would serve 15 years in Otisville prison.

For his help in targeting drug dealers, Federal Prosecutor Rudy Giuliani had Barnes sentence reduced from life in prison to 35 years.

Leroy "Nicky" Barnes is currently in the Witness Protection Program.

*   *   *

On December 31, 1974, as the world awaited with great hope and anticipation the arrival of the New Year, 5,000 police officers, from near and afar, stood at attention in front of St. Gabriel's church in East Elmhurst, Queens as a 29 year old hero police officer, Kenny Mahan, from the 41ˢᵗ Precinct in the Bronx, a Vietnam veteran, was being carried into the church where he was baptized to receive a last goodbye. His wife, Linda, and their 3 year old daughter, Melinda, followed closely behind him, supported by his parents and sister, Michelle.

It was just after midnight on December 28, 1974, while I was home snuggling warmly against my wife in Co-op City that Police Officer Kenny Mahon was gunned down, not by the robbery suspect he sought, but by a criminal with a .357 Magnum, who thought Kenny was coming for him.

While I tossed in bed, Kenny's frantic partner, Mike Black, while returning fire, put his finger into the enormous hole in Kenny's chest in a futile attempt to stop the bleeding.

Suddenly awake and unable to sleep, I went downstairs for a smoke as Sgt. John Battaglia, Joe Spagnola, Joe Kelly, John Santos and Bob Gardner ran under fire across that huge courtyard on Southern Boulevard and carried the mortally wounded fellow officer to their car and sped to Lincoln Hospital.

As I fell back into a deep sleep in that warm bed not many miles away, Kenny Mahon expired on a hard, narrow cart surrounded by doctors and nurses and a tear filled room of men in blue.

The New York Post and page one of the New York Times accurately reported the details of this tragedy. Since my account wouldn't change their stories, nor provide additional solace for those who loved Kenny, I'd rather just report what I wrote at the time.

Tragically last week, Kenny Mahon, who had a gold shield in his future, made the supreme sacrifice for the people of New York.

There's no earthly way to measure this loss, only in heaven can these things be measured. How do you measure a friendly smile, a kind word, a pat on the back, a dry joke, a helping hand? We all knew Kenny as a man, and the death of any man you know diminishes you. We all knew Kenny as a good man, and the untimely death of a good man is always a tragedy. We all knew Kenny as a good man, a good cop, a good husband and father, so surely this tragedy diminishes not only us, but all peace loving people in this city. He made a difference, you all do. May he rest in peace.

However, I'm sure that all of us who were in the Four-one Precinct at that time would like to thank the following:

P.O. Kevin Henry, P.O. G. Torres Jr., and Det. Richard Robinson, all assigned to the 40th Precinct, for capturing the shooter, David Navado, on the roof of 500 Southern Boulevard.

Reverend Bill Kalaidjian for assisting Frank Macchio in the notification of the event to Linda Mahon. Reverend Bill has always been there for all of us—he is, indeed, a special guy.

Burton Armes of the 7th Division Homicide for his work on the case. (Murder 1- arrest # 40618). He would go on the great success in Hollywood.

Inspector Edward Stoll who made sure that all the I's were dotted and T's crossed.

Ed Arrigoni—For his generosity in providing several buses to transport Kenny's fellow officers to the funeral.

And to all those there who helped-you know who you are.

On July 21, 2003, the Mahon family was notified by the Division of Parole, that David Navado was no longer in their custody — he was now deceased.

From Ann Landers

This poem was pinned up on a bulletin board, by an officer who was eventually killed in the line of duty. The source of the poem is unknown. It was sent to Landers by an officer from Raleigh, North Carolina.

A Part of America Died

Somebody killed a policeman today and
A part of America died.
A piece of our country he swore to protect.
Will be buried with him at his side.
The suspect who shot him will stand up in court,
With counsel demanding his rights,
While a young widowed mother must work for her kids
And spend many long, lonely nights.
The beat that he walked was a battlefield, too,
Just as if he'd gone off to war.
Though the flag of our nation won't fly at half mast,
To his name they will add a gold star.
Yes, somebody killed a policeman today,
It happened in your town or mine.
While we slept in comfort behind our locked doors,
A cop put his life on the line.
Now his ghost walks a beat on a dark city street,
And he stands at each new rookie's side.
He answered the call, and gave us his all
And a part of America died.

Kenny will not be forgotten. I've been informed that on June 18, 2011, a street in the Four-one Precinct will be named after him. (See appendix B for the 1974 annual precinct report.)

CHAPTER 6

▼

The number one problem in New York City at the beginning of 1975 was the fiscal crisis. Mayor Beame was struggling to keep the city afloat.

In the Four-one Precinct we were in a more violent battle trying to contain the Savage Skulls, Seven Immortals, Savage Nomads, Brotherhood, Turbans, Roman Kings and yes, The Peacemakers – and 21 other gangs that called Fort Apache their turf.

Sergeant Craig Collins wrote an excellent book, "Street Gangs— Profiles for Police", which documented this gang activity. Of the 336 gang related homicides in the city, between 1971-1975, 152 had taken place in the South Bronx; for rape, it was 132 out of 281.

There was one gang related case that would haunt us for the next two years. And actually, it had started on July 26, 1974.

A badly burned and decomposed body was found in the basement of an abandoned building on Fox Street — it had been there for several days. The Four-one detectives responded. Detective Ken Fowler, a crafty old timer, smelled homicide right away. The detectives checked with missing persons — a kid missing from the 4-3 Precinct fit the description of the body. They visited the boy's father, Mr. Gibaldi, at his job and requested the name of the family dentist, assuring him that it was routine.

Sadly, the teeth of the deceased matched the x-rays of Mr. Gibaldi's son Anthony, a 17 year old who shined shoes at the corner of Southern Boulevard and Westchester Avenue.

Detective Fowler interviewed Banjo Jim, a blind black man who played the banjo while blowing on a harmonica, held by a neck brace, at that location. Jim told Detective Fowler that Anthony popped "reds" but that he was a good kid.

Detective Fowler and his partner went to the Gibaldi home in the 4-3 Precinct and delivered the tragic news. The family was devastated. The mother cried, "This is why we race from the fascists in Italy—for this?" The father was silent.

The detectives then went to the Medical Examiners' office. The M.E., Dr. Pearl, found Phenobarbital in Anthony's blood, but classified the cause of death as "undetermined, no violence found".

The detectives were stymied. They proceeded to the funeral parlor and told Mr. Gibaldi the results of the autopsy. He was upset, especially about the drugs. "It was murder, murder, I tell you", he moaned. The detectives asked him for some information, some clue, some lead that they could pursue, because, if none existed, the case would be closed. Mr. Gibaldi walked away from them into the undertaker's office. The detectives followed.

Mr. Gibaldi looked at the detectives, turned to the undertaker and said, "Replace the wood casket with a steel one". The case was closed.

On November 30, 1974 Detective Fowler received a call from Police Officer Moses of the Equal Opportunity Section. Moses stated that he had been told by an AJ that Anthony Gibaldi was a murder victim. Detective Fowler contacted AJ who stated his information source was "confidential". The story AJ told was that Anthony Gibaldi had been robbed by an Arce Santiago and three others, and because of Anthony's testimony, they were convicted. The father, Mr. Gibaldi, insisted on prison time, so the perpetrators did eight months. Santiago was bent on revenge, and after he was released from prison, he killed Anthony Gibaldi and burned the body to make it look accidental. Mr. Gibaldi was interviewed by Lieutenant Montagnino. Mr. Gibaldi had nothing to offer but parental intuition about the death of his son. He insisted that Anthony was a good, hardworking boy, but was a slow learner. Once again, N.Y.S.I.I.S. was checked and no connection was found between the deceased and Santiago.

In April of 1975 Mr. Gibaldi again contacted Lieutenant Montagnino. The Lieutenant and Detective Bernard Duffy spoke to AJ who admitted that his source of information was Arnold Gibaldi, the brother of the deceased. Lieutenant Montagnino interviewed Arnold Gibaldi who stated that an unknown youth, a few days after Anthony's death, told his brother, Vincent (male, white, 14) that Anthony had been killed. Arnold Gibaldi stated that the family did not know who the youth was, had never seen him before and had not seen him since he spoke to Vincent.

Once again, Lieutenant Montagnino had a check made of the criminal record of Santiago to see if there was a connection between Santiago and the robbery of Anthony Gibaldi. No connection was found. The Medical Examiner was contacted and the findings on Anthony's autopsy remained unchanged. The 41st Precinct Investigating Unit was again left without any firm leads and was unable to move the case. Mr. Gibaldi was informed of the status of the case.

In late June of '75, I spoke to Captain Slattery about the case. I brought two things to his attention:

1. When I worked in the Photo Unit, we always checked with the Bureau of Criminal Identification (B.C.I.) at 400 Broome Street if there was a problem, because B.C.I. was keeping back-up fingerprint files in case N.Y.S.I.I.S. went down.

2. It might be a good idea to have someone check the records at the Bronx Criminal Court.

On July 3, 1975, Mr. Gibaldi made a complaint at the Civilian Complaint Review Board that the Four-one squad hadn't done a proper investigation on his son's death.

Shortly thereafter, Captain Slattery and Lieutenant Montagnino uncovered the fact that Arce Santiago had two N.Y.S.I.I.S numbers and that, yes, Santiago had robbed Anthony Gibaldi receiving a one year jail sentence, but only serving 8 months.

Captain Slattery was annoyed, "I'm going to get to the bottom of this, once and for all. These people have been lying, just lying all the time".

After a review of the case file, Captain Slattery contacted Mr. Gibaldi and asked that he appear at the 41st Precinct with all four of his sons. Mr. Gibaldi came in on July 19, 1975 with only three sons, and they were interviewed by Captain Slattery. They were Oscar, 16; Ensio, 17; and Arnold, 21.

The interviews were conducted in two parts. Each boy was first questioned privately by Captain Slattery. They all said that Anthony was a "good boy," but Oscar, who knew Anthony best, after some time admitted that Anthony had all the faults of any other human. In addition, Oscar had a list of Anthony's friends, and he knew who the "unknown youth" was who said Anthony had been killed. Later, all were questioned together, and it became apparent they had been less than honest until this time to protect Anthony's good name.

Detective Fowler was called in and information was taken in greater detail. It was found that Anthony went with the Savage Skulls, a youth gang in the South Bronx, and that KB, a male, white, 17, had told of the circumstances of Anthony's death.

Lieutenant Montagnino reopened the case again, and with Detective Fowler interviewed KB on July 20, 1975. KB said his information came from "street talk". This was the first source outside the Gibaldi family to claim that Anthony Gibaldi had been killed.

Close cooperation between 41st Precinct Investigating and 41st Precinct Anti-Crime personnel was arranged to gather information whenever a Savage Skull had contact with them. On August 12, 1975 Police Officers William Coyle, Arthur Murray, and John Marchesi, of the 41st Precinct Anti-Crime Unit, arrested "Big Fish," a male, Hispanic, 18 years old, for rape first degree. They informed Detective Fowler that Big Fish was a member of the Savage Skulls and the detective questioned him about the Gibaldi matter and the rape.

Big Fish disclosed that the Savage Skulls had an execution squad, the "Gestapo", of which he was a member. The "Gestapo" carried out a $600 "contract" to kill Anthony Gibaldi for Santiago. He described the torture, stabbing, shooting and burning of Gibaldi. He also gave information on a total of five homicides, an arsenal of 24 guns, a robbery of a gas station and a rape.

Bronx Assistant District Attorney Dembin came to the 41st Squad office and took Big Fish's statement. Assistant District Attorney

Dembin appeared before Bronx Supreme Court Judge Joseph Cohen on September 5, 1975 seeking a court order to exhume the body of Anthony Gibaldi. Judge Cohen granted the order after hearing the arguments and obtaining the consent of Mr. Gibaldi.

The body was exhumed on September 8, 1975 from its grave at the Gate of Heaven Cemetery, Hawthorne, New York.

A re-autopsy was performed at the Medical Examiner's office on September 12, 1975 by Dr. Michael Baden. The cause of death was changed to "Traumatic Asphyxia; Post Mortem flame burns of body; Homicidal".

The M.E. remarked that the only reason he was able to make his findings was because of the steel casket and that the rope marks on Anthony's private parts (as mentioned in the Big Fish statement) were preserved by the fire, frozen in time so to speak.

Mr. Gibaldi cried hearing the news, "Thank God he was gone before they burned him".

The 8th Division Homicide squad with the help of Detective Fowler had put together the corroborative evidence required to bring Santiago to trial (in New York State, a person cannot be convicted solely on the testimony of an accomplice, you need some independent evidence).

On October 18, 1976, Arce Santiago was convicted of the murder of Anthony Gibaldi and sentenced to life imprisonment.

As to Mr. Gibaldi's Civilian Complaint:

Captain Slattery recommended that Mr. Gibaldi's complaint be closed and classified Exonerated for the following reasons:

1. Mr. Gibaldi, for his own reasons, wanted to protect the good name of his dead son, Anthony. He never supplied the 41st Precinct Investigating Unit with the information he had relative to Anthony's lifestyle.

2. The Gibaldi family knew who had told them of the circumstances of Anthony's death but denied it until it was dragged out of Oscar Gibaldi by Captain Slattery.

3. The Gibaldi's knew who Anthony's friends were but never said a word until questioned by Captain Slattery.

4. The unfortunate clerical error of having Arce Santiago's records split under two NYSIIS numbers prevented an early connection of Santiago and Gibaldi.

5. The first Medical Examiner's report indicated that the cause of death of Anthony Gibaldi was undetermined and not due to violence. It did not disclose any cause of death.

A final note: The Gibaldi's have moved out of the Bronx.

CHAPTER 7

▼

Basically, 1975 was divided into two unequal parts, although each was six months long. It was sort of a schizophrenic year—one half didn't want to listen to the other half.

The first half was ridiculous, kind of weird, spooky, and maybe even had a "Rocky Horror Movie" feeling to it.

The second half was emotionally draining, definitely comparable to a death in the family, and maybe, as some suggested, a mercy killing.

But let's start at the beginning.

The first order of business in 1975 was to address the safety of our officers. I sent the following U.F. 49 to Chief Bouza at the borough office on January 10, 1975.

Subject: Issuance of Light Weight Bulletproof Vests

1. The issue of bulletproof vests has once again been brought to my attention by the unfortunate death of Police Office Mahon.

2. It is my opinion that if these vests would save one police officer's life per year, then they are worth the expenditure.

3. It should be noted that Los Angeles has just equipped their officers with these vests. The cost for their 7,000 man department was 7000 times $50.00 per vest for a total of $350,000.

4. The total cost for our department would be approximately 1.5 million dollars. While the initial outlay may appear large, the net cost to the city for a 20 year officer would be $2.50 per year/per man, a most modest figure. There are also city expenses connected with the death of an officer (benefits, etc.) not the least of which is his replacement. Of course, there is no way to cost-out the loss of one man to his family and comrades.

5. For your consideration and action.

Inspector Joe Sampson was writing U.F. 49's too. This one went to Captain Bill Tracy, C.O. of the 42nd Precinct on January 14, 1975.

1. I read with great interest your invitation to attend the first inter-precinct swimming meet to be held in New York City. Your command is to be congratulated on setting up this fine event. A personal note: I have watched with great admiration your personal growth since arriving in the Bronx and taking command of the 42nd Precinct. The 42nd Precinct, traditionally one of the most hazardous and difficult precincts to administer, has blossomed under your innovative and courageous leadership. Your style and verve has inspired not only the superiors in your own command to rise to higher levels of consciousness, but many superiors in other commands, my own Tom Walker included.

2. It was therefore, no surprise to me when this invitation arrived. It represents to me just one more example of your ability to move into a socially disorganized area, an area that is on its knees, and to move it ever upward towards full maturity. I know that the sacrifices that you and the men of the 42nd Precinct have made will not go unnoticed when the final accounting comes due and I will willingly stand with you then; but Saturday, January 25, 1975, is my regular day off.

Yours in Dedication

Joe Sampson

There were two officers whose sobriquets for me (the men had more colorful nicknames for them) were "The Invisible Man" and "Astroman". These officers were an immediate concern for me.

The Invisible Man advanced so many amazing accomplishments, so many incredible adventures, and so many non-traceable encounters with criminals that we decided to check his veracity.

Accomplishments- He won a Combat Cross (2nd highest award) in his last command. Hyperbole—he won an excellent police duty (lowest award possible).

Adventures- Was a prisoner of war in Vietnam. Spent one night in an army brig in Georgia (right, the one just north of Florida).

Criminal Encounters- Yes, he had some real bad situations and was heroic, but so many were invisible, unable to check, sniper fire, etc. Inspector Sampson transferred him to the perfect command for a man with his talents—The Movie Unit.

Astroman was a young officer who had many issues, most of which were generated by either drugs or alcohol. After he threatened to kill me, he was referred to Monsignor Dunne's program for substance abuse (mostly alcoholics at that time). If you asked where this program was held, you were told, "The Farm". Was there really a "Farm"? I really don't know. I couldn't ask Astroman, he never came back.

One lesson I had learned in the Four-one Precinct was that you should never prejudge a situation until you have all the facts.

As Sherlock Holmes once shouted to Watson, "It's a capital mistake to theorize before one has data"!

And so it was when I arrived at the Four-one stationhouse on March 26, 1975. As was my routine, I first stopped at the muster room desk.

Sergeant Savino welcomed me with, "Had a shooting last night. We fired 16 shots, super's apartment, 1821 Bryant, he's D.O.A."

My mind jumped into alert status. "16 shots, basement apartment, 16 shots. Don't sound good", I told myself.

"You have a copy of the report?" I asked.

"D.I. Priestley is having it typed up at the 4-0. I sent a car to pick up a copy. "

"Thanks Sarge, I'll be in my office. "

Sergeant Al Mason, the first supervisor on the scene last night dropped in to see me.

"What happened last night? 16 shots?" I asked.

"Clean shooting Cap, 4 guys, 16 shots."

"Who were the shooters?"

"Schwartz, Kayne, Corcoran and Fox."

"Fox", I wondered, "I thought he was Eileen Degnan's partner?

"Degnan and Donnelly were covering the alley."

"All good guys, but how do 4 cops become shooters in a basement apartment?"

There was a knock on the door. It was Sgt. Savino with D.I. Preistley's report. I took it and he left. I turned to Al. "Thanks Al, let me read the report. I'm sure it will satisfy my curiosity.

"I'll be around, if you need me," he offered, and headed for the door.

The report read in part:

Angel Vega (16), stated that he was shot at by one, tentatively identified as Gil Barreto, the superintendant of 1821 Bryant Avenue because he was jealous of the complainant's attention to his girlfriend. The complainant stated that the perpetrator was now in the basement apartment with his girlfriend.

The officers knocked on the apartment door, received no answer, but heard someone moving around inside.

Officer Schwartz kicked open the door: He entered the bedroom and observed a male standing by the window. He then called to the male stating, "Stop, Police." The male took about two steps to the right and went behind a dresser. The male later identified as Mr. Barreto then pointed a gun at the officer. The officer fired one shot and Mr. Barreto fell, knocking over the dresser. The perpetrator then fired two shots at Officer Schwartz, who fired five more times at the perpetrator. The three other officers standing near the bedroom door also fired. Officer Fox fired six rounds, Officer Kayne and Officer Corcoran each fired two rounds. The girlfriend was on the bed during the entire incident. She corroborated the Officer's story.

The issue of the location of the four officers upon firing still wasn't clear to me. Since I would be doing the I.O. 118 follow-up investigation, it had to be determined.

Time-Out- I'm jumping from 1975 to February 4, 1999, the night that Amadou Diallo (born September 2, 1975) was killed. What follows is a note I sent to a friend who was interested in the case (which I hope will also clear-up any question the reader might have about the 1975 shooting)

Trish,

An old 41 Precinct case, I handled the follow-up investigation. If I did one of these, I did a hundred!

Important

A). 1975) 4 officers – 16 shots with .38 specials. 2 emptied their weapons – 6 shots each; 2 fired 2 shots each. One officer reloaded. Officers fired 16 or 24 possible shots or 2/3rds of capacity.

1999) 4 officers – 41 shots with Glock 19 revolvers. A Glock 19 standard has 15 shots. Possible shots, 60. Officers fired 41 of 60 possible shots or approximately 2/3rds of capacity.

B). In 1975, we fired first believing perp had gun in hand (he did in 1975 case). In Diallo case officers believed he did—he didn't, he held a wallet.

C). There was initially some concern at Headquarters over the number of shots fired in '75 until all the facts were known – Fox and Schwartz were in the 10 foot by 17 foot room; Corcoran was kneeling in the doorway; Kayne was standing by the left door jamb.

D). Each fired the number of shots based on individual evaluation of personal danger. (Fox and Schwartz in the room fired 6 shots — they were in greatest danger).

In Diallo case - 2 officers testified that they believed Mr. Diallo was pointing a gun at them. (It was a wallet) Another officer testified that he fired to protect his partner.

E). The key to the Diallo case is why was that first shot fired- not the 41 shots. The 41 shots can be explained by the technology, the number of officers confronted (unusual to have 4 officers in shooting position), psychology of self-preservation and situational background.

And yes, as was the Blackrock shooting, this was a tragedy.

All the best,

Tom

Back to 1975

D.I. Priestley concluded his report as follows:

This investigation reveals that all officers involved in this shooting acted to preserve their lives within the guidelines of I.O. 118 and are to be commended for their courage and intelligent action. Recommend assignment to Bronx Area Administrative duties until further orders.

In 2000, all four officers in the Diallo case were found "not guilty" by a mixed-race jury in Albany, New York.

My family has been in the N.Y.P.D since the Civil War. Cases such as these affect you deeply and make retirement look exceedingly attractive. As Chief Bouza stated in his book, "Bronx Beat", "scenes like Fox Street and Fort Apache take the starch out of you".

If the chief contemplated retiring due to his occasional visits to Fort Apache in the 70's, you can imagine the effect on officers who patrolled these same South Bronx streets everyday.

*   *   *

In April of 1975, Spring 3100 noted the following:

In early April the men and women of the 41 Precinct in the Bronx dedicated two plaques to the memory of fallen comrades: PO Kenneth Mahon, killed in December 1974 and Det. Joseph Picciano, slain in February 1971.

The ceremonies, attended by the Police Commissioner and ranking Department officers, members of the community and the officers and supervisors of the Simpson Street station house, included a memorial Mass concelebrated in the sitting room by Father Louis Gigante and Father William Smith. The vestments worn by the priests at the Mass were also donated to the church by the officers of the Four-one Precinct.

*   *   *

A U.F. 49 from D.I. Sampson to the Chief of Operations dated May 8, 1975

1. Summons # 51 533088 5 was issued to vehicle driven by Captain Thomas J. Walker, Operations Executive, 41st Precinct under the following circumstances.

2. Captain Walker scheduled for a 1300-2100 tour of duty on May 8, 1975 finished some personal business in Manhattan and at approximately 1210 hours was driving across 14th Street when he observed two police officers, surrounded by a crowd, attempting to subdue a rather large individual opposite 245 East 14th Street. Captain Walker stopped his vehicle and assisted Police Officer Puccio, shield # 30806 and Police Officer Pattison, shield #30782, both of the 9th Precinct, in subduing the individual. After being assured by the two police officers that everything was under control, Captain Walker left the scene and returned to his car where he found a ticket for double parking on his private vehicle. The time was approximately 1225 hours. He then drove to the 41st Precinct and signed in at 1255 hours.

3. In view of the circumstances wherein Captain Walker had halted his private vehicle to assist two fellow police officers, I ask that this summons be voided.

*   *   *

I told P.O. Nick DeBrino, a scooter summons man, about getting the summons. Nick said, "You're talking to the wrong guy Captain. I hate double parkers. That's why I joined the department. I love giving those tickets. You deserved it….Sir".

I started to laugh. Nick had found his niche.

*   *   *

A midnight to 8 a.m. tour — The Rookie.

Neil Lorenz's specialty was spotting stolen cars, but tonight he hesitated— he promised to take his wife to the doctor in the morning. The rookie badly wanted a GLA arrest. The kid promised he'd handle all the paperwork and take the guy to court in the morning.

Neil spotted a Chevy outside a drug location. "There's one," he told the rookie.

Neil tells the story:

"Wait here, until he gets into the car and then pull up next to him and block him in. The rookie stops short of the mark. We're out of the car. The thief accelerates his Chevy and tries to run the rookie down. The rookie fires one shot. It breaks the windshield but bounced past my ear. The Chevy slams into another car and now I'm in a foot race. I capture the guy. A citizen approaches me, he's bleeding. "A cop shot me!" he claims. It's a glass cut. I showed him the one I got on my arm. It was a nightmare. With all the interviews, the paperwork, the arrest, etc., I worked through the day tour. Yes, the rookie got his GLA arrest. I saw Elinor, Dolores and Denise, three of my favorite civilian clerical folks and begged them not to assign me that rookie again. They all laughed. I inquired, "Why?" "That rookie," said Denise, "just asked us the same thing about you!"

*   *   *

June 14, 1975

There are no heroes in this police story—no princes—only villains and victims. But who were the real villains and who were the real victims? That's what this story is all about. For me it started in 1972 in the 41st Precinct in the South Bronx.

I'm the Operations Officer, a lieutenant. I read the roll call, head down, eyes on the onion skinned paper. A voice responds to the name yelled out. Each name, if you've been in the precinct long enough, triggers to mind a capsule cliché: hairbag, lover, chisler, good cop, boss fighter, etc. Ultimately, unless something extraordinary happens, your relationship with the cop behind the name will be strictly governed by that mental tag. It makes life easier. You can't get to know 460 guys personally—and in this precinct you probably wouldn't want to.

Each tour has a life of its own: births, deaths and everything in between telescoped into about eight hours and fifteen minutes. It's not heaven and it's not hell—it's earth, the Bronx. The only exit you have is time. There's no Gods and there's no devils—only people, some good and some bad. But each tour, however reluctantly, some cop is destined to assume the Lord's role. And every cop dreads the day it will be him. That night it was a guy named Bill Milo. A psycho tried to gun him down. Milo killed him.

But that's not what I remember most about that tour-life. It was the name Ryan—I had to reclassify it. It annoyed me. I was comfortable with Ryan—Kid Hero. Yes! The sobriquet was partially derogatory. I liked the hero. The kid irritated me.

That night Ryan-hero had rescued a 5 year old Puerto Rican boy from a fifth floor ledge by racing in and out of an inferno that had been an apartment. Three hours later, at four in the morning, Ryan-kid was in the muster room exchanging empty milk container fire with his partner, Finnegan—unmotivated, friendly.

I was on meal relaxing in my office. The noise startled me. An attack on the Fort? I lumbered to the rescue. As I reached the desk, Ryan-Kid was near the archway, his arm raised in catapulting position. I acted instinctively. I slapped him across the face. Silence. Everyone had turned into blue marble. Now—I froze too. Lieutenant slugs cop, I thought; a great way to make captain. Finally, I yelled, "Get back to work." The stationhouse came alive again.

As I left the precinct at 8:15 that morning, Ryan approached me. He apologized. I tried to do likewise but he wouldn't hear me out. "No harm—no foul" was all he kept saying. I finally got the message. Ryan knew that I had been alarmed by the muster room cacophony and was rushing to an imaginary rescue attempt that his mischievous efforts had inspired. In his mind, he had been the offending party and since he felt the punishment fit the crime, he just wanted to forget it. I was more than happy to agree. Ryan-Kid Hero was replaced by Ryan-O.K. Cop. O.K. Cop would become the first New York City Police Officer ever convicted of homicide in the line of duty.

Shortly after the night I reclassified him, Tom Ryan left the 41st Precinct. I didn't lose track of him completely — Spring 3100 made sure of that. That Police magazine chronicled his exploits as a member of the Department's football team—a tough victory over the Fire Department, followed by a trouncing of the outclassed inmates of Greenhaven.

The following summer Ryan was inducted into the Police Department's Honor Legion (a select group of officers rewarded with that designation for bravery in action—sounds like war—right, folks?). Billy Rath—Top Cop, ran into him at the Celtic Café that fall. Ryan was still single, Billy reported. We shook our heads knowingly. It made married cops happy that Tom remained so—it was the rationale we used to let him lead the charge when needed. Then came that night—June 14, 1975.

Ryan, now assigned to the 44th Precinct in uniform, responded to 1030 Nelson Avenue, the Bronx, to what appeared to be a burglary in progress. Two cops at the scene had already seized three men they suspected of the burglary (3 guns and a bag of money in their possession). One of the men (Mr. Santiago) made some comments about a Mr. Rodriguez who lived on the second floor. Drugs, money guns? As Mayor Koch says, "So what's new?" Ryan went to investigate. He knocked on the door. The response he received was a bullet. Ryan the hero emerged (wearing bulletproof vest). He pushed in the door, charged the man with the gun and tackled him. Sam Huff had never done it any better. How could this ever result in Ryan being charged with homicide? Let's hear from Ryan again.

"A drug dealer shoots at me. I don't shoot him. If I did, I'd be a hero. Instead, I tackle the guy. I'm not gentle with him. He tried to kill me. But I didn't abuse him. Look, what's the sense of talking? The poor guy lay in the hospital for four hours with a ruptured spleen before they even tried to help him. Someone had to take the rap. I was the arresting officer. I admitted subduing the guy. If I was responsible it would be easier. It's tough. That's why I jumped bail and disappeared for two years. I was innocent. I couldn't see going to jail for something I didn't do. In retrospect, I guess I should have stayed and fought it. But after the accident in Manhattan and the Appellate Division ruling against me, I lost all hope. But it was still a mistake to run. I don't mind paying for running away. But the homicide! Well, you know what I think about that. You know what the jurors thought too."

What the jurors thought, too? He must be kidding. Well, let's humor him. Here's Marie Bischoff. She was on the Bronx jury that listened to all of the evidence in November of 1977. Marie, didn't you find Tom Ryan guilty of homicide?

"I do not believe that Thomas Ryan was guilty of homicide in any degree and in no way caused the death of Rodriguez by kicking and punching the deceased in the home or at the station house. Ryan did use force in subduing the deceased but did not render undue force. I also believe that we had four separate charges to consider. If I had kn that Criminal Negligent Homicide was under the first indic Murder 2, under no way would I have voted for Crimin Homicide. I would have voted for acquittal all the wa

Strong stuff? Here's another juror, Elizabeth C

"After listening to all the evidence I firm' Ryan was not guilty of Homicide in any de

Rose Sammartino has something to say:

th
indic
conti

"I am of the firm opinion that Thomas Ryan is not guilty of Homicide in any degree. I misinterpreted the charges. All I thought was negligence—not homicide. I would and could not, with all my heart, convict Mr. Ryan of Murder or Manslaughter or Homicide. When Judge Tonetti came up to the jury room after our verdict (which we did not understand) we asked what this was and had no idea this Criminal Negligent Homicide was part of Murder. I thought, and so did others, that this was a very minor charge—negligence. Mr. Tonetti said we did pick the lesser of the charge, but we said "Not murder," and he said the verdict would stand as is. Had we been allowed to vote when we went back to the jury room, I was prepared to vote "NOT GUILTY" on the charge of Criminal Negligent Homicide and acquit the defendant of all charges. To me, the most misleading part of the whole ordeal was the slip of paper or charge, whichever one, and how the charges were listed. Such as:

1. Murder #2, or
2. Manslaughter #1, or
3. Manslaughter #2, or
4. Criminal Negligent Homicide.

Now when we were given this paper as marked above, how in the world were we all to know the charge of Criminal Negligent Homicide was under murder?"

Yes, here's another juror, Mary Ann Gorrasi:

"The misunderstanding that arose from this trial, I blame on the sheet presented to us by Judge L. Tonetti. It read as follows: 'Murder #2 or Manslaughter #1 or Manslaughter #2, or Criminal Negligent Homicide.' As the deliberation got under way, I, nor any of the jurors, in any way, or at any time did find Thomas Ryan guilty of Manslaughter#1, Manslaughter #2, Murder #2 or Criminal Negligent Homicide. Again, may I say that I and the other jurors were grossly misled by Judge Tonetti's presentation of the indictment and derivations. Had I known that Criminal Negligent Homicide was under the first part of the indictment of Murder #2, I never would have voted guilty. I would have continued with my stance of acquittal. The second time we were sent back to the jury room, by Judge Tonetti, to reconsider, I would have taken my position again for acquittal. I feel Judge Tonetti was most unfair in sending a court officer up to dismiss the jury, before we even had time to reconsider our positions. Immediately after Judge Tonetti came up to the jury room on our request, I and the other jurors told him of our gross mistake. I screamed and yelled, telling Judge Tonetti that Thomas Ryan was not guilty of murder or homicide in any degree."

John J. Corbett, the foreman of the Jury, had similar thoughts:

"The jury, as a whole, misinterpreted the indictments against the defendant Tom Ryan. If we were allowed the time for further deliberations, I definitely would have gone for an acquittal. This is in reference to the last time we were sent up for deliberations. At no time during these deliberations did I think that Mr. Ryan was guilty of any degree of murder. This was written in my last note to Mr. Lawrence Tonetti, but was never delivered because of the time element. The Judge at this time had sent the court attendant up to tell us that he, the judge, had accepted the verdict as it was given. I think this was a grave mistake as this was not the intention of the jurors."

Juror Herman W. Rudder:

"After we gave our verdict, Judge Tonetti then caught us by surprise by stating that the charge was related to the charge of Murder 2nd Degree. I and most of the other jurors would not have reached this decision if we suspected that this was so. I myself would have voted not guilty under the circumstances."

John Hall said, "I do not believe he was guilty of homicide of any degree."

The negligence some jurors attributed to Ryan was that he left his prisoner alone in the apartment and responded to a ruckus on the roof of the building. They also believed that he didn't keep a close watch on his prisoner in the stationhouse.

What do you think? Has justice been well served in this ʳ know how I feel. Let's ask Ryan.

"I'm distraught now. I thought the Court of Appeals wʳ I was shattered by the conviction. I started drinking. ᴵ never drank before that. Everything was going dᵒ

Tom Ryan, then 33 and still single, had taᴸ cons say, for the entire incident. He was sentence years. I wish I could say to all of you, as Ryan had said to me in 1972, "No harm—no foul," but he had been harmed and there's no referee to yell, "Foul!"

Tommy Ryan served his time (saved a few guards from injury while doing so) and is presently, a very happy guy, living the "good life" by the sea.

*   *   *

While Tommy Ryan was in Riker's Island prison awaiting trial, his father died in upstate New York. Corrections Commissioner Ben Ward refused to let Ryan attend the funeral.

Ryan's lawyer, Edward Dudley, wrote an impassioned brief, but it did no good.

Louie Palumbo and I refused to let it stand. We went to night court on a Friday with Dudley's brief and spoke to Judge Rothwax about the situation.

The Judge agreed to release Tommy into the custody of Billy Rath — Top Cop, as long as we promised to have Ryan back at Rikers Island on Monday morning. We agreed.

At 2:30 a.m. on Saturday, I heard a voice in our courtyard yelling, "Captain Walker, Captain Walker, where are you?'

It was Tommy Ryan.

We welcomed him and shared a cup of coffee with O.K. Cop and then he was gone. Top Cop was waiting outside for him. Mary smiled saying, "You and Louie did good" and hugged me.

*   *   *

The beginning of the second half of 1975 was fast approaching.

The P.B.A. signed an agreement with the City for a 6% raise, effective July 1, 1975. In return the cops were giving back some days. It never came to pass.

Mayor Beame, the bookkeeper, had failed to save the City — it was going under. For years, the City had spent more than it could afford.

On July 1, 1975, 38 thousand City workers, including 5,000 police officers (every cop hired from 1969-1974) were chopped unceremoniously om the City's payroll. In the Four-one Precinct we lost 69 young, dworking officers. It was devastating. 26 Firehouses were closed, in the Four-one.

So much of the rhetoric of that year sounds so familiar today, as we struggle with the 2011 fiscal crisis.

Tony Bouza said of the 1975 layoffs we should "Adopt a Poisonous Weed program a la Chairman Mao rather than indiscriminately firing the most recent arrivals!" Seniority is still under attack in 2011. There was also a cry to crack down on excessive pensions and welfare in 1975.

We hear similar cries today. I'm not so sure that eliminating seniority and returning to the "spoils" system is the answer. Do we want the politicians and bureaucrats making the hiring and firing decisions? Now they want to establish a "merit" system. To me, merit is just a 2011 code word for "spoils", "quotas" and "diversity!"

There's two simple ways to solve the problem:

1. Balance the budget every year.
2. Get union rules that allow municipalities to fire lousy workers.

Then the last in first out (L.I.F.O.) problem will be non-existent and we'd have true diversity—one based on opportunity and ability.

Good luck!

1975 was a heartbreaking time. We had to collect the guns, shields, and I.D.s from all those disenchanted officers. It was tough. We lost all five of our female police officers.

There was one officer who couldn't bring himself to comply — Robert Bilodeau. Bob rationalized his refusal with "Maybe it's a mistake — not me".

Finally, he was the only officer left on the list. With no choice left, I sent a Sergeant to Bob's home to pick everything up.

Bob's distraught wife, Kathy, was there. Bob, a tear in his eye, fin complied.

It had been so emotional for the Sergeant, he avoided rest of the day.

I never forgot that day. I never forgot Bob. That e itself indelibly on my soul.

When Bob was re-hired, he left the Four-c that his throat had been slashed while working i.

disguised as a derelict. He survived, but I worried about the guy — he was fearless, a cop's cop. And the S.C.U. — what a unit. They were using "Compstat" methods before that computer based program was born (one year they took over 900 guns off the street). My friend Trish was one of its stars.

Bob received the Medal of Honor for that near death experience.

Then it happened. On February 12, 1980, in the 28th Precinct in Harlem, Bob and his partner spotted a man with a gun. The man, a predicate felon out on bail ordered by cut-em-loose Bruce, ran into an alley. Shots were fired. Both men were hit. Both went to hospitals. Bob died at Harlem Hospital. The killer had escaped but was captured at a Mt. Vernon Hospital. He is now serving a life sentence.

I went to the wake (I was retired then). Many friendly faces from the recent past greeted me. A Sergeant was there too— yes, that sergeant. We shook hands. We both understood. There was nothing much that needed to be verbalized. He just said, "I knew you'd be here". And I nodded.

I went to the funeral.

Policemen mourn such losses publicly. The only other time we get noticed by the law-abiding public is when we hand out a traffic ticket. But this isn't sour grapes. The death of another cop offers an intimation of your own mortality and you tremble a bit more.

So you wear your best uniform and you stand in a sharp blue line. You hoist the heavy coffin, covered with black crepe, and bear the contents toward a narrow hole in the ground. And then when you stand up, you realize that half your prayers were made for yourself. For it is only when you stand in that long blue line, outside some chapel you probably never saw before and hope to God you'll never see again, living or dead, that you realize how alone you are.

You also remember as the rain beats down (for some reason it always rains those days) those that died in battle. The subsequent litany is depressing but necessary, and one by one you'd say a prayer for each and every one of those murdered cops. Bob was awarded a second Medal of Honor — the first officer ever to receive such a tribute.

On July 1, 1975 the P.B.A. had thousands of officers in front of City [Ha]ll with signs saying, "Beame is a deserter. A Rat. He has left the City defenseless". Then they marched over the Brooklyn Bridge during rush hour. It got nasty—tires were deflated, bottles were thrown, etc.

Fear City became Stink City when 10,000 Sanitation workers walked-off the job in protest of the layoffs.

Libraries were closed and free tuition was ended at all City Colleges.

The anger, the demonstrations, the nastiness just wouldn't stop.

Governor Carey created the Municipal Assistance Corporation (MAC) to help sell City bonds. Felix Rohatyn was put in charge of the Emergency Financial Control Board to make sure the budget was balanced. It was tough and it would take a couple of years for the city to become solvent again.

At the time, I wrote a letter to the editor entitled, "Where does the street cop fit into this mess?"

"The street cop has seen his buddies fired. He has taken various pay cuts and not received the raises negotiated for him. However, raises are granted to his superiors and the members of other departments. He sees other departments re-hiring, while his laid off friends continue to suffer. He is represented by an organization that is leading him in a negative direction both economically and intellectually. His wife is upset being caught in an inflationary period with diminishing resources. He is forced to work a chart that takes him away from his family for an additional 10 days. His hope of promotion has been shattered by the fiscal crisis. On top of all that he must still be able to handle a tough and dangerous job. As each days passes, he becomes more angry and more frustrated. Strangely enough, most have given the P.B.A. leadership a pass as to why they have been mistreated. Sadly, an equitable solution to the pay dispute cannot be attained until the power struggle within the P.B.A. is resolved. A union must speak with one voice. In the meantime, as usual, it's the cop on the street who suffers."

*   *   *

On October 28, 1975, my mother-in-law, Kathleen F↗ Delany, passed away. She was a wonderful Irish lady, al↗ help any of her four lovely daughters. We would all m↗ on St. Patrick's Day. Her verve for the holiday an↗ prepared always left us singing her praises. Go↗

Yes, it was a depressing time, both personally↗

*   *   *

At times, the matter of a policeman's life is beyond Reverend Bill Kalaidjian's mortal powers. Then he must carry-out his grimmest obligation — notifying a cop's wife that her husband is dead — he has done it over two hundred times.

It was Christmas. The Police helicopter had gone down in the East River. The pilot's body was missing and would not be found for three days. Bill remembers saying, "the poor guy had two kids."

Bill went to the house in uniform and rang the bell. Through a window, he could see Christmas tree lights blinking in the living room. An ashen-faced woman opened the door carrying a blond baby; a three year old stood next to her.

"Was it his helicopter?" was all she asked. Bill said, "Yes".

"I'll turn the Christmas lights off," she said.

"No, don't do that", said Bill, "He wouldn't want you to upset the kids any more than necessary."

She smiled knowingly, as tears streamed from her blue eyes and down her freckled cheeks, and then she fell into Bill's bear hug.

In 1975, Reverend Bill was ordered to the 41st Precinct by the Police Commissioner at Christmas time to give a lecture on corruption. This, to a group of men and women who had just lost so many of their brother and sister officers to layoffs. On top of that, these young cops were probably the most shot-at and discouraged group of men and women in New York City history.

Well, Bill did mention corruption, but by the end of his talk there was not a completely dry eye, an untouched soul, an un-elevated spirit or a cop there that did not believe that they were doing God's work and that the good folks of New York did care and appreciate their heroic efforts (it was my first meeting with the force, cops call simply, "Reverend Bill" — and the start of a friendship that has lasted since that first meeting).

It was an uplifting end to a very bad year.

CHAPTER 8

▼

In 1976, as Fort Apache burned, the city continued to close firehouses in the area. It was a disaster. Ever since the Cross Bronx Expressway was constructed cutting the borough into two separate and unequal parts, one north and one south of the road from hell, the deterioration of the Bronx was assured.

As property values in the South Bronx fell and the City began to cut subsidies which had helped to stabilize the area, a scandalous, frightening and inevitable slide into oblivion was set in motion.

Initially, as building owners abandoned their property and frustrated tenants moved north, squatters and street gangs moved in, accelerating violent drug-related crime and escalating the arson problem.

As the slide into pandemonium rapidly advanced, both the owners and tenants developed more sophisticated strategies.

If you were a tenant and you wanted Social Services to move you out of Fort Apache, there was a simple solution-- burn out your apartment or even better, burn down the whole building (less obvious).

When Engine Company 82 responded to these alarms, the residents had already evacuated the building and had their furniture and belongings neatly packed sitting on the sidewalk. As one resident told me, "You do, what you have to do."

Bankrupt building owners were also doing what they had to do -- they sold their buildings to a "Finisher."

The Finisher would strip the building of everything of value (pipes, fixtures, wiring etc.,) sell the loot, and then burn down the building for the insurance money. It was a lucrative business.

One morning, Police Officer Dolan arrested two Finisher helpers with a truck load of plumbing, wiring, toilets and other fixtures. The lieutenant at the desk, destined to become the Chief of Personnel, told the officer to wait until he returned from lunch to book the culprits and voucher the truck.

The officer waited for an hour and 15 minutes until the lieutenant returned. There was only one problem. When the officer went to the street to obtain some information required by the lieutenant, the truck was gone.

The lieutenant wanted to give the officer a complaint—I vetoed it. I admonished the lieutenant, "you should have done your job first and then taken your meal. (Cops on the street do it all of the time). I.A.D. was called and responded (I didn't invite them).

I was blunt, "If you give a complaint to the cop, I'm giving one to the lieutenant". Eventually, the battle was deemed a draw and the matter dropped.

In 1989, the lieutenant, now the Chief of Personnel, assisted me to insure that my daughter, Mary Anne, would become the first 5th generation police officer in the NYPD and not a first generation cop in the Transit or Housing P.D.s.

It was a magnanimous gesture on his part. Maybe, that's why he made chief and I never received a non-civil service promotion.

However, in 1976, my life was going to be consumed by outside forces, events derivative of the publication of my book. Personally, it would be an exciting and career altering year.

(For a complete look at the 41st Precinct roster as of January 14, 1976 see appendix C)

I had finally completed the manuscript for my book, tentatively entitled, Fort Apache-- the Four-one Precinct. The Thomas V. Crowell Co., an old (1834) and venerable book publisher, showed some interest. I was excited, delighted and cooperative. It was suggested that the book needed some editing—it was too "harsh". A female writer was brought in to make it more "sensitive"—it was a disaster. I rebelled and refused to accept the changes. The deal was precariously close to dissolving. Moe Devito gave me some good advice, "Go easy with these people.

Literary folks are cut from a different cloth than we are". I asked and was granted some additional time to edit the manuscript.

I contacted a writer, Rodger Huehner, who had loved the original manuscript. I asked for his assistance. Rodger edited it, taking out most of my beloved dashes, adding some comas and periods, and eliminating my dangling participles. He did a great job. I re-submitted the manuscript to Crowell.

At the same time, a seasoned and well respected agent, Theron Raines (James Dickey of Deliverance fame was one of his authors) read the manuscript and agreed to represent it. A deal with Crowell was quickly struck. That accomplished, Theron immediately started to explore other revenue streams.

In early February, Theron called to tell me that New York Magazine was interested in doing a piece on my upcoming book.

"That's great, Theron. Good Work", I offered. Theron, a phlegmatic professional, just cleared his throat and said, "They want to talk to you. It's either going to be Fort Apache or King Kong on the cover of the February 23rd issue".

"That's amazing," I injected.

"A photographer will be coming to the precinct. Please coordinate it", he concluded.

"Yes, sir," I happily replied.

Three days later, I headed for Second Avenue in Manhattan. Sitting with several editors and writers in the magazine's busy copy room discussing the issues confronting both the officers and residents of the Four-one Precinct was enjoyable—someone really wanted to know the particulars of life in the South Bronx.

As in acting, making a speech or in teaching a class, when the performance is over, an independent evaluation of your performance isn't required—you know. In this case, I nailed it. We were getting the cover.

On February 23, 1976 New York Magazine hit the newsstands. The cover, illustrated by Julian Allen, was thrilling, electrifying and just plain sensational.

It pictured the Four-one Precinct stationhouse punctured by a dozen arrows (the feathers of the barely seen 12th arrow provide the illusion that the Fort is surrounded). The headline, "Siege of Fort Apache" in bold red letters immediately grabbed your attention.

The next day, as I was exiting the stationhouse, Chief Bouza was standing there examining the building.

"Tom, I don't see any arrows", he said, in good humor.

"I made sure that they were removed before you saw them chief," I replied, with a chuckle.

Tony smiled, nodded and entered the stationhouse.

I wasn't sure how the department would react to the article. The magazine displayed photos taken inside the stationhouse as well as in the field. I'm certain that some internal discussion on the matter transpired, but honestly, the only direct comment was that just described exchange with Chief Bouza.

However, the response of the community leaders was, well, less than gracious.

A typical response was encapsulated in the following letter (and there were a few) to New York Magazine (and I never used the word "animals"!):

Siege Mentalities

May I state that I am deeply disturbed by Captain Walker's article, "The Siege of Fort Apache" [February 23]. While Captain Walker speaks of violence and youth gangs in Fort Apache, his article contributes to and reinforces a typical white, suburban view of those people who live like animals in "those places in horrible New York City."

I have walked the streets Captain Walker describes, and I find here a tough vibrant, living community, a community that desperately needs help-- assistance that has not come forth either from the Housing and Development Administration of New York City or from the South Bronx Model Cities Program. A major part of the 41st Police Precinct is located within the Community Planning Board #3 District. This community has been consistently forgotten.

Captain Walker's article is typical of the New York City Police Department's siege mentality and of its long-term inbreeding. I imagine that the New York City police officer who works at the 41st Precinct can go home after his tour of duty, confident that he is driving home to his suburban $40,000 home, secure that "they" will never reside in his neighborhood....

Paul Muscillo

Neighborhood
Community
Renewal
Corporation,
Bronx

I responded to the letter as follows:

Paul Muscillo's emotional retort to excerpts from my book ["The Siege of Fort Apache", February 23] in the March 15 Letters column was partially misdirected. He attacks the one agency that has truly attempted to meet the needs of this community -- the Police Department. I also refuse to accept his holier-than-thou posture.

I grew up in the Bronx and still live there. So do many other police officers. Some do live outside the Bronx, as do some community leaders. If Mr. Muscillo equates living outside the Bronx with unresponsiveness to community problems, he is misguided. If my book helps to focus attention on an area long forgotten by our city, state and federal agencies, as Mr. Muscillo acknowledges, I will have been successful.

Tom Walker
Bronx

*   *   *

April 1, 1976

It came as a shock to our family -- Jack Faherty, Mary's father, had passed away only 5 months after his dear wife, Kathleen, had expired. Father Tolienti said it was a sign of how much he had missed and loved her.

Jack had worked as a laborer on the Empire State Building, had opened a bar, "The New Manhattan", on 3rd Avenue in Manhattan with the Mullarkys, then sold it years later and opened the "Celtic" on Castle Hill Avenue in the Bronx. It was the grandest wake I've ever attended— folks from every borough showed up—fishermen, bar owners, patrons, and drunks he had brought home who had no place to spend the night. Yes, he was a simple God fearing and humble man—and his daughters were cut from the same cloth. You did good Jack.

I was thankful that Jack had seen the New York Magazine article and had enjoyed it. I sensed that he now knew that his lovely daughter, Mary, was in good hands.

*   *   *

Things slowly quieted down. It was late April and the Yankees had returned to the Bronx to a renovated Yankee Stadium. I was delighted when Inspector Jesse Peterman, a low-keyed and sharp boss, invited me to join him as the guest of Ed Arrigoni in box 324 at the stadium. It was a welcomed break.

Ed Arrigoni, the President of New York Bus Service operated the largest and most efficient express bus operation in the city, employing over 500 drivers and mechanics, and transporting daily over 22,000 North Bronx commuters to Manhattan. What was to be a one game guest appearance quickly turned into a lasting friendship of 35 years. In 1983 Ed established the "CopShot" Program—it provided a $10,000 reward for information on culprits who shoot at cops.

At this point, I'd like to share with you four of the most gratifying and emotional visits that I participated in at the House That Ruth Built in the Bronx. (Being in suite 324 was definitely a participatory event).

*   *   *

This was more than a sporting event. It was, in one sense, a religious experience.

August 7, 1979. We had just returned from Canton, Ohio from Thurman Munson's funeral to play Baltimore. It had been an emotional roller-coaster. We were in 4th place, 15 games out and going nowhere, but there were 37,000 fans here praying for some mystical sign from the gods that Thurman was safe at home. It didn't have to be a grand miracle, just something to hang our hearts and souls on, just something to exorcise the stark reality of a young man's death, just something to restore our faith in baseball's ability to transcend mortality, to insure immortality.

We're losing 4 to 0 in the 7th. Bobby Mercer hadn't hit a homer since his return from Chicago on June 29th, hadn't hit a homer in Yankee

Stadium since September 28, 1973. Dent walked, Willie Randolph doubled and then Bobby hit one into the right field stands. The place went crazy. Dr. Alfred Lowy said, "Don't worry, the gods are with us tonight."

It was 4 to 3 and it stayed that way to the bottom of the 9th. Again it was Dent, Randolph and Bobby. Dent walked, Randolph got a bunt single. Tippy Martinez wild pitched them to second and third. With two strikes on him, Mercer went the other way, lining a single to left scoring Dent and Randolph.

All hell broke loose. The fans were delirious. Mercer jumped into Yogi Berra's arms. The whole team converged on home plate – you'd thought they'd won the World Series, but it was bigger than that, they had won it for the Captain, Tugboat, Thurman Munson. The universe was at peace again.

*   *   *

August 16, 1982

Ed called at lunch. He was upset. "We're dead." He said. "I don't even think corked bats will help. They even got to the Goose. Oh, well what the hell – we can still have a few drinks and some laughs at the suite tonight."

The White Sox had gotten to Gossage for four runs – it was the biggest insult so far in a season of insults. Poor Guidry will never get that 12th victory. He had pitched well, but then so had Morgan and Righetti. Losing 3 out of 4 to Chicago had dropped us to eleven out. We needed a streak – a long one. It didn't appear likely with K.C. and Gura coming into town.

I arrived at the Stadium at 5:15 p.m. for the twilight doubleheader. Mel Allen was in the lobby. "Bill White had a little accident," he said. "Nothing serious, but they want me to do a few innings on radio." We got into the elevator. "How's Rizzuto's wrist?" I asked. "Broken I hear", he said. Then he chuckled – that sweet Alabama laugh that his listeners so dearly loved, and added, "I better be careful going home." Mel said that he would stop by Ed's suite for a drink after his stint. Tonight's guests were in for a treat. It was kindness extended by both Phil and Mel because of their friendship with Ed. It was incredible to watch the effect that Mel and Phil had on even the most sophisticated guests. The old were made young and the young were made respectful – the latter being more incredible that the former. For me, it was always a thrill to talk baseball with two of my childhood hero's. How about that? Holy cow!

Another great night. It was the first time I ate dinner in the suite. Roast beef, angler fish, beans and rice followed by carrot cake and coffee. Later we had a snack – dogs, ice cream, popcorn, pretzels and more dogs. And of course, a few beer. Willie Nelson had left behind some Lone Star talls which we happily guzzled. The Yanks won the first game 2 to nothing. Righetti was superb. Mazzilli homered. It was as simple as that.

The pitching carried the day, but we would still only be an illusionary contender if our hitting didn't come around – and soon. Winfield is in a slump – 0 for 15 or 16. Goose got a save. Nice to see him get over that Chicago business so quickly.

A solitary figure sat in Steinbrenner's luxury box – it was Richard Nixon. The President had the entire suite to himself, except for his secret service detail. He watched the game intently, as his protection ate ice cream. Mel Allen, after talking to Ed, went to ask the President to join our party. I was struck by the kindness and thoughtfulness of my companions. Upon reflection, I understood. Ed, a fervent Democrat and complex man, had a carefully disguised love for fallen warriors. He loved nothing better than watching a discarded slugger come through in the clutch. Yankee history is filled with such men – pennant drive acquisitions like Johnny Mize – who rose to the occasion and led the Yankees to victory. And more than anything, Ed Arrigoni was a Yankee – a believer in that tradition: be a gentleman, be a winner. I looked at him, wondering if my evaluation was correct. Then I saw it – for cripes sake – that guy was wearing a blue suit with white pinstripes. Mr. Yankee himself. Mel Allen, the Voice of the Yankees, added another dimension. Mel, back on top again, like Nixon had once suffered a fall from grace – leaving the Yankees after our defeat by the Dodgers in the '61 series. His voice, some claimed, had cracked in disbelief as Koufax delivered the coup de grace. Mel had fallen from power – the power of the Yankees announcing booth and all the adulation and prestige that went along with it. In the years that followed, Mel had done well –two books, numerous credits (NBC and now Cable) and just recently, the

Victor award, confirming his rise, once again, to the top of his profession (he's in the Hall of Fame too). Characteristically, Mel's voice cracked and his eyes watered as he delivered a simple but eloquent acceptance speech in Las Vegas. It's the nature of this emotional and sensitive man that his voice will always crack when he cares.

The President declined our invitation, but insisted that we join him. Irv, owner of Prestige Plaques, grabbed his camera and with Jeannie Arrigoni, Ed's delightfully playful oldest daughter, sprang out of the suite with Ed trailing the pack. A gracious President posed with each of us for a picture, including my daughters, Cathy and Ellen.

The President sat next to Ed in the first row while Mel and I sat directly behind them to facilitate the conversation. We were all a little surprised with the possible exception of Mel Allen – The President was one hell of a baseball fan. "If the Angels get John," he said, "They could go all the way. It would be a bad move for George – everyone has known about Kisson's problem for a long time." He talked about West Coast baseball from '36 to the present. He was good baseball company. I asked if he had heard President Reagan's tax speech earlier that night. He had. He reflected on how well Reagan spoke. "One could never tell that he was using a teleprompter," he said. He seemed more interested in the technique than in the substance. The '60 debate with Kennedy crossed my mind. "It was a good speech," The President said, smiling, "But he'll have a tough time selling it." We left the President the following inning. What had started as a mission of mercy had turned into a rich remembrance. For each of us brought away a little of the youthful American dream – any kid can grow up to be President. We had just met a kid who did.

Mel, Ed and I had a drink while re-hashing the President's audience. The President had said that he didn't have much athletic ability. He mused that if he had to do it all over again, he would like to be a sports announcer. Ed, politically astute, wondered if Reagan's speech has affected Nixon that deeply. Reagan, he pointed out, had started as a sports announcer.

"I was surprised that the President admitted those things," I said.

A distant voice at the bar said, "It's the only thing he has ever admitted." Camelot dissolved – we were back in the real world. Nixon's latest book, "Leaders", was due in the fall. He promised to send Mel a copy. I decided to buy a copy – I liked the guy.

Sitting here at the typewriter, I can't remember if we won or lost the second game. And for some reason, it doesn't seem that important.

*   *   *

June 21, 1990. It was a pleasant June night in New York City. In the Bronx, Yankee Stadium was rocking with 55,000 joyous celebrants.

The crowd, overwhelming black, was there to join a New York salute to Nelson Mandela. Mayor Dinkins, sworn in as New York's first black mayor six months earlier, would lead the celebration.

The stage area, set up in left field near the 318 mark, was swarming with federal and local security forces. Local politicians, celebrities and of course Mandela's entourage.

In suite 324 high above home plate sat the families of the Bronx borough president, the US congressman representing the South Bronx, the wife of a local Cadillac dealer, a white political science professor, Denise Rivera and a couple of other commissioners. I was the host that night.

At the rear of the suite stood two retired police detectives watching in professional silence. I walked back and asked them how it was going. The word coming back to them via their earpieces was that the crowd was well behaved and happy—always a good sign.

The Bronx Borough President, Freddy Ferrer, was on the stage making a welcoming speech. When he returned to the suite a short time later, with 4 NYPD Community Affairs Officers in their blue jackets, they reveled in how they were able to get through the intense security to the stage. According to their reports, Jessie Jackson had been unable to get past State Department officials and up on the stage.

Mayor Dinkins did his best to stir the crowd (after chiding them for booing the mention of George Steinbrenner's name and his generosity for waving the 90,000 dollar rental fee for Yankee Stadium)

The Mayor, a phraseologist of note, was at his best tonight. The professor loudly shouted his approval.

But the major happening that night was produced, as it should have been, by the guest of honor.

Nelson Mandela, still an unknown entity to most New Yorkers, made an immediate connection with everyone in attendance that night.

Taking the microphone, he donned a New York Yankee baseball cap and, with a big grin, announced, "I am a Yankee."

The Stadium went wild.

The two old security officers at the rear of the suite smiled and applauded too. They were men not easily fooled or raised to enthusiasm. They looked knowingly at each other. I smiled too and applauded, as I nodded to them in agreement.

This was a man, this Nelson Mandela, to bring people together, not to divide them. This was not a man of hate. He was truly, a man of hope. History has confirmed it.

Remembering Nelson Mandela that evening, as I write this, reminds me that there are phraseologists and then there are those leaders with dignity, intelligence and biblical wisdom who speak of universal truths from their hearts.

*   *   *   —

October 26, 1996. The night we beat the Atlanta Braves 3 to 2 in the 6th game of the series, coming back from an 0 – 2 game deficit to win 4 straight incredible games, and capture the World Series Title.

The next day, I sent this note to Ed.

It was definitely a very special night. No doubt, the greatest sports event at which I've been present.

One could sense at the outset that something extraordinary was about to take place. Only later would I realize that it was the crowd that conveyed that message – it oozed with verve and confidence.

My ordinary Murphy's Law mentality vanished with Gerardi's triple – only then was I completely in tune with the crowds' optimism.

The game was tense and well played, but it was the communal experience, the emotional charge generated, that set it apart from other nights we shared behind home plate in suite 324.

All too often in the suite, the game is overshadowed by celebrity – the Dick Nixons, the Willie Nelsons and even the Joe DiMaggios. On those nights, I remembered their presence, not the final score, not the opponent. But not this game.

Al D'Amato, Mario Biaggi, and Bobby Mercer were welcomed but minor distractions. My focus never strayed – it was wonderful, pure. The game was the thing.

Life is a bumpy continuum, but it's nice that some things never really change.

With that in mind, it was gratifying to share this marvelous October night with a fellow lover of the game. For that, I thank you.

Tom

P.S. and I nearly scooped that foul ball with the net!

AMERICAN PIE

Here it comes, letter high, fast and hard
Not a Ryan or Reynolds, but a roaring Welch
The spinning sphere, tumbling violently
A bee-bee, a pea, a bullet blur at 140 F.P.S.
Only 60.6 feet to fly.

Suddenly, frenetically, hopefully
A labeled oak thrusts high to meet it
To interdict the path prescribed to catcher leather
The two just kiss – no full embrace
No violent splash – no echoed thunder.

A ricochet on line toward backstop screen
A crowd scream does erupt
The batter jumps to check the flight
Oh, what might have been
The catcher and the ump recoil
Yes, another foul ball.

To those above in three – two- four
The drama's just beginning
For perched with nets sit elderly gents
The ball is their desire
The missile dents the web of giving wire mesh
Thus, its backward rush absorbing.
Slow motion now prevails – old reflexes
Versus Rawling decelerating, screen –hugging ball
The old men rise, as knees crack
The showdown has arrived
Their youthful quest for this honored guest
Brings thoughts of ages past.

Of meadows green to summer's Good Humor chocolate ice cream
To dreams of life unfolding
Of apple pie and favorite girls
The old men never tire

It matters not if win or lose
The speeding sphere they're hunting
The memories its approach has triggered
Are all that really pleasures

The nets are thrust – their metal hoops clang
The men, they push and shove
They parry and laugh and revel
In amusing ineptitude

Their moves have slowed, the eyes deceive
The missile it eludes them
The day is saved by youngster green
Who sweeps from suite adjoining

The crowd erupts as sagging net
Is raised in triumph now
The old men cheer and quickly sit
Their failure undetected.

They cheer the youth in booth next door
Their celebration unencumbered
Another ball, another day
These wise men – they know the score
They talk of other days and deeds
And each enjoys a cold Coors beer

Young Welsh is set and once again
The drama is beginning
Will Reggie raise October Pride?
And send the sphere aflying
Or will the wishful guest in three –two- four
Get another shot.

They tense and watch this endless plot
So simple yet enduring
A man with ball – a man with bat

The dance of pitcher – hitter.
A civilization at its best
A gentleman's survival test
Welcome, my friend, behind home plate
To Big Ed's – three – two- four.

CHAPTER 9

▼

On May 1, 1976 my book, now entitled, "Fort Apache – Life and Death in New York City's Most Violent Precinct," arrived in book stores on the east coast – it was considered a regional book by the publisher.

It was an emotional day for me – joy, relief, a creation coming to life after a long and difficult developmental process.

The publisher had 200 copies delivered to the Four-one Precinct. The precinct's Four-one club sold the books at a reduced rate and added the monies so collected to their treasury.

I happily sat in my office and autographed books, adding something special about each officer for the entire tour.

Once again, there was no official response to the event. To be honest, I was oblivious to any problems the book might create – I saw it as a positive for the residents of the precinct.

Donna Gould, a dynamic, non-stop publicist at Crowell, had arranged a score of appearances on radio and T.V. shows:

Television – On Sunday, May 9th, Eyewitness News Conference on channel 7.

May 17th – Midday Live on channel 5

May 18th – AM New York on channel 7

Radio – The Joe Franklin Show, The Barry Grey Show, The Barry Farber Show, The Candy Jones Show, etc.

As I entered the stationhouse early on the Morning of May 6th,

Mario Giasoni, our Administrative Lieutenant, a big smile on his face, sauntered in my direction waving a paper.

"Hey Cap," he shouted, "You were reviewed in the Times."

I couldn't believe it. "You're kidding, The New York Times?" I queried.

"The same," he replied.

Of course my follow-up question was, "Did they kill me?"

"No", Mario said, "It's not bad."

Mario was right. I was more than pleased with Anatole Broyard's review (Years later Mr. Broyard's life would be depicted in the movie, "The Second Stain").

Here are some excerpts from the review:

THE NEW YORK TIMES, THURSDAY, MAY 6, 1976
Books of The Times

Reality on the Fire Escape
By Anatole Broyard

Fort Apache, by Tom Walker. Edited by Roger W. Hushner. 195 pp. Crowell. $7.95

On more than one occasion in "Fort Apache:" police officers running up a fire escape in the South Bronx to confront an armed suspect on the roof of a building have noticed that quite a few people were looking out their windows at the "show". It was better than television. The man or men on the roof might be suspected of murder, felonious assault, robbery, rape or arson. When the police finally cornered them, as they often did, it was a question of who would be shot and who would survive, but some of those at the windows did not seem to care. For them, it was entertainment.

In fact, books are among the most successful products of the "inner city" ghettos. Claude Brown's "Man Child in the Promised Land" and some of James Baldwin's work are good examples. Now, in "Fort Apache," a police Captain, Tom Walker, looks at the ghetto from the fire escape, so to speak. And we ought to be grateful the he does, for the ghetto should also be seen from the point of view of this other group that suffers in it; the police, the public servants.

There will be readers who will question the "objectivity" of "Fort Apache." This is only natural – as natural as questioning the objectivity of the books written by the inhabitants, or former inhabitants, of the ghetto. It is to Mr. Walker's credit that he is not "angry," a priori, at the people in his precinct. He is angry only when they hurt his men or an innocent victim, and unlike other ghetto authors, he keeps his rhetoric to a minimum. He seems to regard apocalyptic statements as shots fired unnecessarily.

Even Mr. Walker, who has now been promoted out of the 41st Precinct says, "It was horrible, it was poignant, it was funny, and it was sad, but most of all it was real." Perhaps all social reforms ought to begin by defining "the real."

*   *   *

On Sunday, May 9th, I appeared on channel 7's Eyewitness News Conference moderated by Milton Lewis, Melba Tolliver and Roger Sharp.

I enjoyed the interview – there was s tough and honest exchange of views. Towards the end of the discussion, Milton Lewis asked me, "There's a proposal to make the top ten floors of the World Trade Center into a "red light" district; what's your opinion? I thought it was a joke – I had never heard of such a proposal (readers, please don't mention it to Mayor Bloomberg).

In any event, my response was "Oh, there's already prostitution on the 57th floor." To me, it was a Freudian slip. I knew who I was referring to as soon as the words passed my lips.

As with Walter, I forgot about it.

Later that afternoon, I received a call from Milton Lewis to inform me that Nadjari's office had called and bitterly complained about my remark about prostitution on the 57th floor. I asked Milton, "What's the remedy?" "They didn't propose one." He replied. "They're a defensive bunch." I thanked Milton for the call and no, I didn't quite forget it. That evening, I decided to watch the 11 o'clock news on channel 7.

My wife, Mary, and I were sitting in the living room as the show opened. The first thing I heard as their theme music dampened was:

"Police Captain claims that there's prostitution in special prosecutor Nadjari's office on the 57th floor of the World Trade Center."

Then they showed a two minute clip of the interview.

Mary was upset. I wasn't happy – I was still waiting to make my required appearance before Nadjari's grand jury.

The next morning, I received a call from the borough office – Chief Bouza wanted to see me.

The chief presented himself to me in his usual pleasant and cordial way. He never said it, but I sensed that he felt as I did – this was bullshit, an overreaction by a bunch of prima donna legal thugs (I'm sure he would have said it in a more sophisticated manner).

I have to say this – I liked Tony Bouza. Okay, I didn't always agree with the self – described "People's Chief", but the S.O.B had cojones and brilliance and craftily used that combination of traits to stick needles into the more pedestrian leaders of the city. He was walking on the edge of a cliff, as was I, and in September, we would both fall off. (Pushed might be more accurate).

What follows is Chief Bouza's May 10th report on my interview to Chief Michelson, the Chief of Field Services.

POLICE DEPARTMENT
CITY OF NEW YORK

May 10, 1976

From: Commanding Officer, Bronx Field Services Area
To: Chief of Field Services Bureau
Subject: APPEARANCE OF CAPTAIN WALKER ON T.V.
SHOW.

1. Captain Thomas Walker, Executive Officer, 41st Precinct, appeared live on a half hour showing of "Eyewitness New Conference' at 1400 hours, Sunday, May 9, 1976. The show was moderated by Milton Lewis, Melba Tolliver and Roger Sharp and emanated from 7 West 66th Street, Manhattan. Captain Walker's appearance was arranged by the publisher of his book "Fort Apache," Thomas Crowell. There was no fee connected with this appearance and it was not cleared

with DCPI. Captain Walker appeared in civilian clothes and was on an authorized excusal approved by Deputy Inspector Ciccotelli. He was there to promote his book.

2. I saw a film clip of the controversial part of the show – running about 2 minutes – on May 10, 1976. This was the segment shown on the channel 7, 11 p.m. News. In this section Milton Lewis suggests the creation of a legal red light district and mentions "why not the top 10 floors of the World Trade Center, with a red light on top?' Captain Walker's answer was, in paraphrase, that there were reports of prostitution in the building and mentioned the 57th floor.

3. The 57th floor of Tower A of the World Trade Center is occupied by the Port Authority. Tower B is occupied by the Special Prosecutor's Office.

4. I personally interviewed Captain Walker on May 10, 1976 at 1530 hours in my office. He appeared voluntarily and contributed the time, although off duty. He made the following points:

a) He picked the floor at random, although his one and only visit to the building occurred three years ago, when he appeared at Mr. Nadjari's offices. He felt the 57th floor was lodged in his subconscious as a result.

b) He made no connection between Mr. Nadjari and the floor, either on the show or in his mind, and neither did any of the other participants. It wasn't until he was called by Mr. Lewis sometime afterwards, in response to a telephoned complaint from Mr. Nadjari's staff, that any connection between the floor, the remark and the Special Prosecutor's Office was made. This call from someone reportedly representing Mr. Nadjari apparently inspired the far more sensational reporting that appeared on the 11 p.m. News.

c) Captain Walker stated he'd been a bit non-plussed by Mr. Lewis's proposal – not having given the matter much thought – and, thinking there already might be prostitutes plying the building, made a lame attempt at humor. The connection, he felt, is unfortunate, regrettable and unintended. Captain Walker specifically stated that he intended no slur on Mr. Nadjari or his staff.

5. Under the circumstances, the sensitivity of the Special Prosecutor's Offices is entirely understandable, even though neither his name nor his office were named on the show in question. This is a regrettable confluence of coincidence, sensitivity and tasteless humor. Captain Walker was appearing as the author of a book, although he was identified as a member of our department and must, of course, behave accordingly.

6. Captain Walker regrets any misunderstanding that may have arisen from his inadvertent and subconscious comment. He intended no slur on the Special Prosecutor's Office. Recommend that that office be advised of the results of my brief inquiry.

7. Respectfully submitted as per your request.

Anthony V. Bouza

Assistant Chief

A few days later, I was subpoenaed to appear before the Nadjari Grand Jury. Was this payback time? Maybe not, but it was time to get a lawyer.

Later that day, I heard that Nadjari had subpoenaed Patrick Cunningham, the Bronx Democratic Chairman to appear before the same grand jury to inquire into the sale of judgeships.

That evening, I went to Dr. John Cahill's office on Seton Avenue in the Bronx for a check-up (John and I had graduated together from Mt. St. Michael H.S. in 1952). I picked – up a magazine while waiting and discovered this disturbing portrayal:

In his "The City Politic" column in New York Magazine, Nicholas

Pileggi wrote a piece entitled, "The Political Future of a Smear Artist." Of course it was about Maurice Nadjari.

What was fascinating about the article was that the Bronx D.A. Mario Merola, a strong supporter of Nadjari in 1973 when he referred me to that office, had done a 180 degree reversal. Here's part of the Pileggi's column:

"Nadjari is a time bomb," one elected city official and former prosecutor said in reference to the prosecutor's ability to slander the innocent. "And the triggering mechanism is a combination of paranoia and whim."

Bronx District Attorney Mario Merola is one of the few public officials who has discussed Nadjari's power to smear. "Of course, he can smear me," Merola told editors and reporters of the New York Times. "He can ruin people in public office. What the hell do you think we've got after 25 years of public office? All we've got is our name, and our reputation, and he can just do it like that [Merola snapped his fingers] to you, even if you've done nothing wrong. "The smear is on the front page and the exoneration is on the last page in the bottom part of the corner. You couldn't be called to the grand jury by Nadjari without being smeared. You just couldn't. It's that kind of an era, that kind of a time that we live in. It's the innuendo, it's the rumors, it's the time, and it's the climate."

In fact, anyone who has ever tried taking on Nadjari has soon regretted it.

My friend, Police Officer Lou Palumbo, the ex-plainclothesman, was checking his sources to find out who else was appearing before this installment of the grand jury. He was informed that the I.A.D.. lieutenant who had worked on the "Walter Case" had already testified. While he couldn't discover the exact testimony (of course, that's secret), he did get snippets – the lieutenant believed that "tape gap" was a "goof" on I.A.D.'s part. That was good news.

My lawyer, Jack Schofield, and I sat in the anteroom of the grand jury waiting to be called. While a lawyer isn't allowed in the jury room when you testify, he can get a sense of where the process is going. Jack had a short conversation with the prosecutor. Then he filled me in on what to expect.

'No big deal," he said calmly, "Just answer the question and abide by the prosecutor's directions." Then he added, "This should be ok."

I was sworn in. I studied the grand jury. Most of them had good eyes. I relaxed.

After the formalities, name, address, etc, the prosecutor asked me about Walter. I thought, "I hate that name". I told the jury about my life with Walter (it felt like a "life" anyway).

I tried to tell the jury about the Bronx D.A, but the prosecutor stopped me cold saying, "We don't need that." We finally got to the key question. "What do you think happened to erase those six minutes?"

I had my own theory – the only one that seemed reasonable. I looked straight at the jury and answered. "After the officers recorded Walter's bribe offer, they came into my office and played the tape. By the way, I never touched the tape recorder. They were going back to record the culmination of the deal. I don't know why or how it happened, but someone must have re-wound the tape to the beginning and then taped over the first conversation."

I then looked at the prosecutor. He nodded and said, "Ok, you're dismissed."

"I'm finished?" I asked. The jury started to laugh. "You're finished, thank you Captain."

Boy, was I glad that was over. It was time to buy Jack and myself a drink.

Yes, reality bites – that night I caught the duty and had to respond to a shooting on Blackrock Avenue (the prologue). Blackrock was the last straw—the cynism of making points on the death of a kid turned my stomach. It was time to retire. I now believe that although Blackrock was the final nudge, the rocky, potholed filled road I had travelled during my return to Fort Apache and my stay there were major contributing factors in that decision.

Later that month, Spring 3100, the department's police magazine reviewed my book. I thought that the magazine editor, M.I. Hofstein, had done an excellent job.

"FORT APACHE"

By TOM WALKER

Life and Death in New York City's

MOST VIOLENT PRECINCT

The eons-old (it seems) adage that every cop in New York City could write a fine book based on his (or her) experiences is probably true. But, sadly, few of us have the presence of mind to properly record these experiences and/or we lack skills necessary to complete the task.

However, Tom Walker – now the Captain/executive officer of the 41 Precinct – saw the potential for a book, an account of his adventures as a newly promoted lieutenant in the early 1970's as soon as he arrived at the 41 and he did something about it.

"Fort Apache" takes us on a roller-coaster ride through the South Bronx, The book is full of first person 'war stories' – many of them fantastic to the point of incredulity – but nevertheless true. If Walker had stopped there, "Fort Apache" would still have been entertaining, causing gasps from here to Peoria. But, he went further.

The book is really about one man's love affair with our police department and about his respect and admiration for its men and women. True, with the telling of the "war stories," Walker extends his admiration to those citizens of the South Bronx who maintain essentially decent lives under horrible conditions, but the captain saves the bulk of his praise for the cops. It is their reaction to the pathetic conditions of the Simpson Street Precinct that continually fascinate him. He is more interested in the expression on the "cops" faces than he is at the discovery of headless carcass of a shaved gorilla at their feet. The description of an especially savage series of unrelated family fights is interspersed with the author's concern for the cop's personal reaction to them. He perceives a "there but for The Grace of God go I' rationale for the cops' moonlighting vigor as stemming from their reaction to the crushing poverty of the South Bronx. It is this approach to the subject that makes Walker's book a good one.

Two further thoughts about the text. "Fort Apache" is not a piece of classic literature...nor, apparently, was it meant to be. It is conversational in tone and is gratifyingly readable. Recently, a major local magazine received an advanced copy of "Fort Apache" and reprinted some excerpts. On the whole, the reaction to the article was excellent but interestingly, a few police officers didn't like it. Maintaining – quite adamantly, in fact – that while the anecdotes were o.k., they objected to them being told by a boss. That's an important criticism – because the false notion that bosses don't get involved with their men or the street dies hard. But we believed that Tom Walker will be vindicated when cops read the entire book.

CHAPTER 10

▼

Donna Gould, Crowell's fiery publicist, had actually read my book and found my interest in Sherlock Holmes most appropriate – crime fiction reflects real criminality.

Donna became aware that the old 64,000 dollar question was to be exhumed and raised up to become the $128,000 Question. Apparently, the word was out in her industry that "experts' in different fields were needed for the show.

Donna called me. "Are you an expert on Sherlock Holmes?", she wanted to know.

"Over the years I've read all of Conan Doyle's works including the 4 novels and 56 short stories about Holmes and Watson," I replied.

"4 and 56" she cried. "You're an expert." Would you like to be a contestant on a new quiz show, the $128,000 Question?

"Why not," I told myself. So I said to Donna, "Sounds good to me."

The show was to be taped in late August to be shown in September of 1976. I had 2 months to re-read those 4 novels and 56 short stories – it became a family project. Mary would randomly thumb through a story and ask a question. "How many steps from Baker Street to Holmes second floor rooms?" My daughter Cathy yelled, "17." "Show off," I countered. Cathy was the math whiz in the family – she never forgot a number. Ellen was entering Fordham College at Rose Hill in September; Tom was a senior and star on the Spellman H.S. football team; John and Mary Anne were still in grammar school. Why did I mention all that? Because it became a major factor in an upcoming decision.

Back in the real world, a bloody horror was about to begin – and it would start in the Bronx. Incredibly, no one would know it was happening until it was nearly half over.

July 29, 1976. It was a quiet, moonlit, Thursday night in the predominantly Italian section of Pelham Bay in the Northeast Bronx.

At 1:10 a.m., two young ladies, Donna Lauria and Jody Valente were sitting in Jody's 1975 blue Oldsmobile in front of Donna's apartment on Buhre Avenue chatting about life.

Suddenly, a man appeared at the passenger side window. He fired three shots from a long-barreled revolver killing Donna Lauria and wounding Jody Valente.

The detectives proceeded as all good sleuths do – everyone was in the circle of suspicion until eliminated. Unfortunately, when the investigation was completed, there was no one left in the circle.

There had been 5 shooting deaths in New York City that night. The figure was expected to reach 2,000 before the year was over. Tragically, many would not be solved. This appeared to be one of them.

In late August, I arrived at the Ed Sullivan Theatre on Broadway between 53rd and 54th street to tape the very first $128,000 Question show. It was a big thrill for me to be on that stage. Sullivan's "The Toast of the Town" was my family's favorite show. It featured the likes of Elvis, the Beatles, and so many other top performers.

The rules of the game were explained to me and the other two contestants for that first show – a female model who was an expert on the Supreme Court and a peanut farmer from Georgia (not Billy Carter) who was ironically an expert on U.S. Presidents.

Each player would select his or her expert category from a game board and be quizzed in the same style as *The $64,000 Question*. The questions doubled in value from $64 to $512, then $1,000 to $64,000. The winners of $64,000 would return at the end of the season to compete for an additional $64,000.

Each contestant who missed a question worth $4,000 or less would end up winning one dollar. A miss on the 8,000 or the 16,000 level would award the player a Buick Skylark. Any contestant who lost on a 32,000 or 64,000 question would end up leaving with $16,000.

Mike Darrow, a pleasant, impressive Canadian-American, was the host. Alan "Big Red" Kalter was the announcer.

I believe I was the second contestant that day – the model preceded me. I was escorted onto the stage by a lovely young lady, greeted by Mike, and was placed into a booth. As best as I can recollect, my second question, for 128 dollars was, "In the Final Problem, what did Watson find at the Reichenback Falls that belonged to Sherlock Holmes". I was presented with 4 answers. I believed that there were two correct answers. Holmes had left a silver cigarette case with a 3 page letter under it by the falls and an Alpenstock (a long walking stick) further back. I honestly don't remember (and have no record) which one I selected. Let's suppose I replied, "The silver Cigarette case".

"Oh, sorry Tom, it was the Alpenstock." Mike said. Before the show we were told that, "If you disagreed with the answer, don't make a fuss, we'll check it out after the show"

I told Mike my problem. He assured me that they would check it out.

I went home that night feeling pretty lousy – knocked out on the 128 dollar question. I just shook my head in disgust. At the next taping, Mike opened the show with this statement;

"On the last show we asked Captain Walker a question. He paused, "Well," he said, as he began to chuckle. "We checked with the Baker Street Irregulars, and they informed us that Captain Walker was correct. So let's welcome back Captain Walker." I did better that night reaching the $4,000 level (At each session, we taped 2 shows).

As the dollar value increased, the questions contained multiples parts. For the $8000, $16,000 and $32,000 questions, if you missed one part of the usual four or five part question, you received a make-up question which you had to answer correctly to advance. Obviously, if you missed two parts of any multiple part question, you were out of the competition. I figured that if you made it to the $64,000 level, you would have answered 24 questions correctly.

Mike always started each appearance with a question for the contestants. The question he asked me on the $8,000 question stands out in my memory.

"It seems strange that a Captain of Police would choose as an outlet a fictional detective".

"Well Mike," I replied, "There's nothing better on a foggy November night than sitting in my room, smoking a cigar, sipping on a coke and reading a Sherlock Holmes story."

Mike was about to reply when I yelled, "or a Pepsi." The audience laughed.

Mike added, "Right, I'm glad you didn't say, I'm going to Disneyland."

I kept moving forward. I was ready for the $32,000 question.

"Ok, here we go Tom," Mike said.

"Sherlock Holmes was a master of disguise. For $32,000. Name the case in which our hero employed the following disguise. One – an elderly master mariner."

"I know this one. It's either The Sign of the Four or a Study in Scarlet." I answered "A Study in Scarlet."

"Oh, sorry Tom, it's the Sign of the Four. I know, you always get those two mixed up."

"Okay, you have to get the next 4 questions correct. If you do, we'll go for the make-up question. Are you ready?"

"I'm ready"

"Two – a drunken groom."

I answered: "A Scandal in Bohemia"

"Correct."

"Three – An Italian priest"

I answered: "The Final Problem"

"Correct."

"Four – An Irish-American espionage agent"

I answered – "His Last Bow"

"Correct."

"Five – a strange, old bookseller"

I answered – "The Empty House"

"Correct, "Mike said with a big smile.

"Alright, let's get to the make-up question. Get this one right and you'll you win $32,000. You ready Tom?"

"I'm ready Mike."

102 Return to Fort Apache

"In which story does Billy, Holmes' page, mention that Holmes disguised himself as old woman?"

"Oh, boy" I said nervously. I then answered: "The Mazarin Stone".

"Correct. You just won $32,000."

The audience, including my wife, Mary, and my daughter, Cathy cheered wildly.

It was a great feeling.

The taping for the $64,000 questioned was the next day – a family discussion was in order.

On both the $16,000 and $32,000 questions, I was able to advance by correctly answering the make-up question. For the $64,000 question, there was no make-up question – it was do or die, and it was a six part question.

If I missed on the $64,000 question I would lose $16,000 and the take home $16,000.

An advertisement in the Daily News for the show displayed my picture with the caption – "Captain Tom Walker can win more than his boss makes in a year."

My ego told me to give it a shot. My five children, three entering college in the next 2 years made a strong case for taking the $32,000. Mary said, "Do what you want to do? I'm with you either way."

I still hadn't decided as I waited to hit the stage the following day. One of the producers, a black gentleman, approached me. "How are you doing?"

"It's tough," I replied. "I'd hate to lose $16,000. He smiled saying, "Go with your gut, Tom. You've been a great contestant." This guy is a mensch, I told myself. He then added, "$32,000 dollars is a lot of money". That conversation sealed my decision.

On stage, Mike Darrow asked for my decision.

"I've decided to take the 32,000 dollars, Mike"

The audience applauded. I looked into the crowd – Mary and Cathy were smiling as they hugged each other.

I tried to deduce what Sherlock Holmes might have thought about my decision. I decided that Sherlock would have been disappointed. Watson might have given me some slack, given my family responsibilities. But, as I've learned in life, you make a decision and you live with it. As time passed, my doubts diminished.

The taping was complete before the end of August. We waited with anticipation for its first telecast on Sept 18, 1976.

I didn't know it at the time, but Chief Bouza's report on my appearance of May 9, 1976 on the Eyewitness News Conference had received its first endorsement by Chief Thomas Mickelson, Chief of Field Services.

On May 11, 1976 Michelson wrote:

Contents noted. The thoughtless remarks and lame attempt at humor by Captain Walker reflect adversely on our executive ranks and the Department as a whole. In view of the ethnically sensitive nature of Captain Walker's present assignment, Executive Captain, 41st Precinct, recommend reassignment where the adverse effects of such undesirable traits would be minimized. In addition, recommend that a copy of this incident be included in Captain Walker's personal folder for career evaluation purposes.

On August 25, 1976, Chief of Operations, James F. Hannon wrote in the 2nd endorsement. "Recommendation has been made that Capt. Walker be assigned to the Communication Division."

In early September, 1976, I was transferred from the Four-one Precinct to the Communications Bureau at 1 Police Plaza in Manhattan.

I wasn't surprised or shocked. Since I was appointed on July 6, 1956, I had completed 20 years and was eligible for an ordinary pension. However, due to my serious vehicular accident (200 stitches in my head) causing a hearing problem, I felt that I should be eligible for a disability pension. A quick decision from the Medical Board, in my case, wasn't in the cards.

*　　　*　　　*

September 19, 1976 was an exciting night in the Walker household as we watched the $128,000 Question. I cringed, but everyone else laughed when I missed the 128 dollar question. The follow-up shows were much more to my liking.

But events were taking shape in the Bronx that would affect my status at the Communication Bureau.

A heavyweight championship between Mohammed Ali and Ken Norton had been scheduled for September 28, 1976 at Yankee Stadium.

At a meeting in Police Headquarters to plan for the fight, decisions were made that negatively impacted the successful policing of the event.

1. Police Commissioner Codd offered to provide Chief Bouza with additional officers, from other boroughs, to help keep order due to the fact that the P.B.A. planned a major demonstration at the stadium – Bouza refused the offer. He would later explain that he resented it when Bronx cops were sent to police events in other boroughs, so he wasn't going to accept any for this event (logical? principled? or foolish?).

2. Bouza refused Codd's offer to have a judge limit the number of police pickets at the event (logical? principled? or foolish?).

The Troops were angry – their agreed to contract hadn't been implemented and 5,000 of their buddies were jobless.

It was imperative that Bouza or his representatives meet with the leaders of the P.B.A. to outline exactly how the demonstration was to proceed, the area(s) designated for grouping, that sufficient P.B.A. Marshals with armbands be present to control their members, etc.

In light of actual events, I doubt that this process had been effectively accomplished.

Bouza's Strategy

He would divide his forces into two groups.

Group one - would handle the usual event necessities—traffic, crowd control, stadium perimeter and a predesignated grouping area.

Group two - Commanded by Bouza himself, this group would meet the demonstrators coming to the stadium from the Manhattan side of the McCombs Dam Bridge.

Apparently, a large group of officers went directly to the grouping area (no senior officer had been assigned there). Now, it got interesting!

Chief Bouza assumed that the behavior of the bridge demonstrators would reflect their prior actions on July 1, 1976, the day of the layoffs, when they blocked the Brooklyn Bridge by walking in the roadway and creating chaos.

Why would he assume this? What agreements had been made at the meeting with the P.B.A.? Had a meeting taken place?

The chief figured that he would confront the mob and threaten them with arrest if they didn't vacate the roadway. He later declared that "I'd force the clash, with me and my staff probably getting knocked on our asses. Whereupon the rest, seeing me and the others getting bowled over, would be sucked into the fray, on my side. Or so I hoped. It was my only hope of effecting arrests, for preventing the night sliding into a demoralizing morass all around, and for simple survival, ethical, professional, and otherwise."

When he saw groups of officers walking peacefully on the bridge walkway to the stadium, "my heart sank" (pg. 29 Bronx Beat).

When he was informed by radio that a large group of officers had gathered at the predesignated and penned picketing site, he dispatched Inspector Heineman to that location (Why wasn't a senior commander there already?).

Heineman reported back that the officers in the penned area weren't content and wanted to parade around the stadium. He claimed that Heineman, knowing his policies, allowed the officers out of the designated area, to march the perimeter of the stadium. What policy was that? The chaos policy?

The chief hurried back to the stadium. He claimed that by 8p.m. he had lost control of the situation.

Sorry chief, this event went south long before 8p.m. on September 28th and yet, despite the folly of his decisions and strategy, the event was salvageable if not for the final mistake – letting the officers out of the penned area.

The combination of officers peacefully walking the perimeter (they did nothing wrong), the huge crowds coming to the event and the "feral" youth gangs ripping off the crowd of tickets, wallets etc. created such confusion (a couple of chiefs alighting from their car including Chief Mitchelson were accidently knocked to the ground) that effective crowd control was impossible.

It was a field day for the media. In the days following the event

Chief Bouza blamed the "feral youth" for much of the problem. In his book Bronx Beat (which I urge you to read to check my account of the event) the chief saw them as "roving bands of youngsters".

The chief's days in the Bronx were numbered. The chief would be cleared of any wrongdoings, but all bosses were required to take a refresher course in crowd control.

Chief Bouza retired on November 26, 1976.

Shortly after Chief Bouza retired, for reasons I have never been able to discover, I was re-assigned to the Bronx borough office. I was home again.

CHAPTER 11

▼

There have seen many excellent books written on the Son of Sam — the best one I've read was by George Carpozi Jr. I was particularly interested in his comments about another case, The Mad Bomber, a case I had critiqued as a young officer and included those findings in my book, "The Demons of Redemption". It took 16 years before the police went public with all the information they possessed on the bomber (1st bomb, 1940—went public, 1956). Were we doomed to repeat that error?

On October 22, 1976, a long haired Carl Denaro was shot in Flushing, Queens, he survived. No connection was made with the murder of Donna Lauria in the Bronx.

On November 26, 1976, Joanne Lomino and Donna De Masi were standing on a Queens Street when a man walked up to them and opened fire with a .44 caliber revolver. Joanne was hit in the spine and was paralyzed. Donna was lucky – she only received a broken collar bone. No connection was made to the prior cases.

On January 30, 1977, Christine Freud and John Diel were in a car in Queens when they were fired upon. Christine was killed. The weapon – a .44 caliber revolver. No official connection was made with the previous shootings, but the local papers were running stories that these shootings were related.

In February, a recovered .44 cal slug found in the car that Carl

Denaro was in when he was shot, added him to the list of .44 caliber shootings.

All shootings involved a man fitting the same description, all were shot with a .44 caliber, 5 shot, long barrel revolver made by Charter Arms – an unusual weapon that was favored in the western badlands by such legendary figures as Jessie James and Bat Masterson. And all the victims fit the same profile – young girls (18-20), with long brown hair (Denaro was mistaken for a girl).

Hey guys let's get real here.

On March 8, 1977, Virginia Vaskerichian was walking on a Forest Hill Street when she was shot and killed. The city and its leaders were just awaking to the unfolding terror.

On March 16, 1977, the police released a sketch of the killer. However, there still wasn't any coordinated response to the killings – The Bronx was The Bronx, Queens was Queens.

Then on April 19, 1977, Valentina Suriani and Alexander Esau were parked on the Hutchinson River Parkway service road in the Pelham Bay section of the Bronx when they were both shot in the head and killed. This time it would be different. Why? Because the killer left a letter addressed to Captain Joe Borelli at the scene. Did we learn anything from the Mad Bomber Case? No! The letter was not released to the public. It would remain the secret of the newly created task force that would operate out of room 224 in the 109th Precinct in Queens.

Did I see the letter? Nobody that I knew in the department saw the letter. Didn't we learn anything from the history of such events?

34 years later it's ok if you see it. It was written in block letters with some lower case letters.

Here is the Captain Borelli letter:

"I am deeply hurt by your calling me a wemon [sic] hater. I am a monster. I am the "Son of Sam." I am a little "brat'. When father Sam gets drunk he gets mean. He beats his family. Sometimes he ties me up to the back of the house. Other times he locks me in the garage. Sam loves to drink blood. "Go out and kill" commands father Sam. Behind our house some rest. Mostly young – raped and slaughtered – their blood drained – just bones now. Papa Sam keeps me locked in the attic, too. I can't get out but I look out the attic window and watch the world go by. I feel like an outsider. I am different wave length [sic] then [sic] everybody else – programmed too [sic] shoot to kill or else. Keep out of my way or you will die! Papa Sam is old now. He needs some blood to preserve his youth. He has had too many heart attacks. Too many heart attacks. "Ugh, me hoot [sic] it urts [sic] sonny boy. "I miss my pretty princess most of all. She's resting in our ladies house but I'll see her soon. I am the " Monster" – "Beelzebub" – the "Chubby Behemouth." The wemon [sic] I love to hunt. Prowling the streets looking for fair game – tasty meat. The wemon [sic] of Queens are z [sic] prettyist [sic] of all. I [sic] must be the water they drink. I live for the hunt – my life. Blood for papa. Mr. Borrelli, sir, I don't want to kill anymore no sir, no more but I must, "honour thy father." I want to make love to the world. I love people. I don't belong on Earth. Return me to yahoos [sic]. To the people of Queens, I love you. And I wa [sic] want to wish all of you a happy Easter. May God bless you in this life and in the next and for now I say goodbye and good night. Police – Let me haunt you with these words; I'll be back! I'll be back! To be interpreted [sic] as – bang, bang, bang, bang, bang – ugh!! Your in murder Mr. Monster."

Would I have gotten a clue from this letter? No! But maybe you or someone else just might have.

The detectives questioned fifty-six .44 Bulldog revolver owners in the city. Ballistic tests ruled out all of those weapons. Stake-outs were employed in The Bronx and Queens. The department, at this point, was doing its best.

Then on May 30th, another letter surfaced. It was sent to Columnist Jimmy Breslin at the New York Daily News. It was handwritten by a person who stated that he was The Son of Sam.

Breslin consulted with the police department. They requested that certain portions of the letter not be published.

Breslin agreed and The Daily News published the rest of the letter a week later. Would any part of this letter have been made public if it was sent to Captain Borelli? I doubt it.

In any event, it was published later in The Daily News, which contained the phrase that I considered important and propelled myself and Lou Palumbo (right, the borough messenger) on our own hunt for The Son of Sam.

Here is the Breslin letter:

Hello from the gutter of N.Y.C. which are filled with dog manure, vomit, stale wine, urine and blood. Hello from sewers N.Y.C. which swallows up these delicacies when they are washed away by the sweeper trucks. Hello cracks in the sidewalks of N.Y.C. and from the ants that dwell in these cracks and feed in the dried blood of the dead that has settled into the cracks. J.B., I'm just dropping you a line to let you know that I appreciate your interest in those recent and horrendous .44 killings. I also want to tell you that I read your column daily and I find it quite informative. Tell me Jim, what will you have for July twenty-ninth? You can forget about me if you like because I don't care for publicity. However you must not forget Donna Lauria and you cannot let people forget her either. She was a very, very sweet girl but Sam's a thirsty lad and he won't let me stop killing until he gets his fill of blood. Mr. Breslin, sir, don't think that because you haven't heard from me for a while that I went to sleep. No, rather, I am still here. Like a spirit roaming the night. Thirsty, hungry, seldom stopping for rest; anxious to please Sam. I love my work. Now, the void has been filled. Perhaps we shall meet face to face someday or perhaps I will be blown away by cops with smoking .38's whatever, if I shall be fortunate enough to meet you I will tell you all about Sam if you like and I will introduce you to him. His name is "Sam the terrible." Not knowing what the future holds I shall say farewell and I will see you at the next job. Or should I say you will see my handiwork at the next job? Remember Ms. Lauria. Thank you. In their blood and from the gutter "Sam's creation".. .44 Here are some names to help you along. Forward them to the inspector for use by N.C.I.C: [sic] "The Duke of Death" "The Wicked King Wicker" "The Twenty Two Disciples of Hell" " John'Wheaties' – Rapist and Suffocators of young Girls. PS: Please inform all the detectives working the slaying to remain. P.S: [sic] JB, please inform all detectives working the case that I wish them the best of luck. "Keep 'em digging, drive on think positive, get off your butts, knock on coffins, etc" Upon my capture I promise to buy all the guys working the case a new pair of shoes if I can get up the money. Son of Sam [18].

If that letter wasn't in the Daily News, I never would have seen it.

For me it was the second name used, "The Wicked King Wicker". I had been told by a detective with the Task Force that there was no deductive way to solve this case. Apparently, others in that group thought otherwise. Until I started writing this book, I was unaware that some detective had seized upon the very same phrase that I did. That detective's hunch was that it might relate to a 1973 movie, "The Wicker Man." A private showing of that movie was arranged for the Task Force. It didn't work out, but I congratulate the detective who thought of it – that's good police work.

My reading of the term was a little different. I sensed that he was the "King of Wicker" or "King of the Hill." It was my hunch that he lived alone (on a hill) on a street that had "Wicker" in its name.

From my studies, I remembered a quote from a Jack the Ripper letter he had written to the London Police, "What fools the police are. I even gave them the name of the street where I live."

I'm sure Jack didn't make it an obvious notation, but most likely hid it in some cryptic phrase.

As panic engulfed the city and young ladies cut their hair (as did my daughters), Louie and I began our search. We hit the local Bronx streets – Wickham and Wickersham. There were no hills of note. We returned to the borough office in defeat.

D.I. Ciccotelli was waiting for us – word of our search had reached his hungry ears. After he informed the borough commander of our "unauthorized activities," we were ordered to cease our investigation.

It dampened our spirits, but we continued, as best we could, on our own time. We didn't have "Google" in those days, so we brought some maps – Queens was our obvious next choice. Louie lived in Whitestone with his wife Anne in a home his father had built in the 1950's on 149th St. – It was a beautiful place. It was our Queens headquarters. Unfortunately, Queens came up negative.

We slowly developed another theory. In any random serial case, wouldn't the first murder be key? Wouldn't the killer pick an area that he found comfortable, that he lived near or worked near? We figured that the guy might actually live where I did – Co-op City. We checked the files of the Coop City Police – no luck (It turned out that he had lived here years before).

On June 26, 1977, Sal Lupo and Judy Placido had just left the Elephos discotheque in Bayside, Queens and were sitting in their car when they were shot. Luckily, their injuries were minor.

Louie and I had checked Pelham, New Rochelle, Mt. Vernon

and Eastchester. It was time consuming, but we came up empty once again.

As July 29, 1977 approached, the Police department mobilized hundreds of officers, many as male-female decoy couples to hopefully capture this madman. On the 29th, Louie and I were sitting in a vehicle near the Shorehaven pool in the Soundview section of the Bronx.

Louie had marked off the shooting sites on a map of the city. If the shooter hit near that pool, it would complete an "S" on the map, with only one more such hit needed in that general area to complete an "S.S." on the map. Nothing happened – this guy wasn't stupid.

Two nights later, he avoided his usual haunts and struck in Brooklyn, killing Stacy Moskowitz and severely damaging Robert Violantes' eyesight.

A parking ticket would lead to the arrest of David Berkowitz on August 10, 1977, outside his home at 35 Pine Street, Yonkers, New York.

It was a sigh heard around the city. The Son of Sam would kill no more!

Beautiful young ladies and their escorts were especially relieved.

Louie best described what happened next.

"I'll always remember that look on Captain Walker's face after checking the Yonkers map and finding a Wicker Street – his rosy cheeks went dead white, ashen." Louie and I immediately drove to Yonkers, which is basically north of the Riverdale section of The Bronx – about 20-25 minutes from Co-op City.

Standing on the corner of Warburton Avenue and Wicker Street, we scanned the area. Wicker was a short block with 4 or 5 houses on the right side of the street, the left side was the backyard of the house on Warburton Avenue, and behind that was a road leading up a hill alongside of a huge retaining wall.

Louie pointed upwards saying. "There". High above the retaining wall I could see an apartment building. We didn't say a word as we drove up the incline to check it out.

I was apprehensive; there was no victory here for me. There was no make-up question that would set things right. This was one page that couldn't be re-written. Mistakes in this business have deadly consequences. I prayed that I was wrong.

At the top of the hill, I turned right and stopped.

"What's the street sign say?" I anxiously asked. Louie got out of the car. I followed.

We looked at each other; we were standing in front of 35 Pine St, the home of David Berkowitz, the Son of Sam.

I shook my head in regret. All those beautiful lives snuffed out. Maybe we could have saved one of them.

Louie was more vocal. "If that son-of-a-bitch hadn't ratted us out," and then he went "Italian" which I didn't understand. But I could tell from Louie's face and tone it wasn't complimentary.

To lose a child is the worst thing that a parent can suffer – Mary and I knew it well. I still say a prayer for all of them. And yes, that feeling of guilt and regret still linger in an old man's soul.

Note:

The house on Warburton and Wicker belonged to Sam Carr who owned a dog and had a daughter named Wheat who was a dispatcher with Yonkers Police Department.

If you care to, re-read the letter to Jimmy Breslin just ahead of where I have it underlined. Does anything strike you? Oh well, I guess Jack the Ripper had a point.

Berkowitz is currently housed in The Sullivan Correctional Facility in Fallsburg, New York. He is serving six life sentences.

CHAPTER 12

▼

As previously reported, I had no clue as to why I was transferred back to The Bronx, but it was well received.

Chief Sachson, an anti-corruption champion nearing retirement, had replaced Tony Bouza. Sachson had an eye problem, glaucoma, and was seeking a three-quarters disability pension.

I had an ear problem and 200 stitches in my head from a police car accident and was seeking the same type of pension. The Chief's chances of success greatly exceeded mine.

Chief Sachson, being Sachson, requested that I do an inventory of all department property to determine if anything was missing.

A week later, I reported that two typewriters were missing. What follows is a spoof of the actual conversation discussing that loss.

To Whom It May Concern:

One week after Chief Sachson was assigned to the Bronx, I, Thomas J. Walker informed him that 2 typewriters were missing from the borough office. In addition to the above, the following conversation took place in his office (transcription of tape recording of that conversation – I used my private recorder)

Chief Sachson – Other than the 2 typewriters, is anything else missing?

Capt. Walker – You mean paper clips and things like that?

S – Tom, paper clips….I mean big things – like a precinct station house.

W – I'm (phone rings)

S – That's right Bouza, two typewriters. No – I enjoy the ride from Bklyn. He did me a favor. I don't know why you're laughing Tony. Yeah, 2 typewriters. Yeah, Walker's here. I don't think they'll fit. Ok Tony – look – right. (Hear bang of phone.)

W – Chief, there's this Herb Miller, a community leader – he's got a typewriter on loan from Community Relations. He's at 169th St. & Grand Concourse, next to the deli.

S – Jewish Deli – 169th St. & Grand Concourse.

W- 169th St. & Grand Concourse. Right! Next to the deli, right!

S – Yeah, I remember that place – good corned beef.

W- I'm not sure. How about Herb Miller?

S – Yeah I don't know the guys name but he makes a great sandwich. Let's see. Yeah it's about that time.

W- Yeah it's about that time Chief. How about a corned beef and a portion of potato salad? Miller?

S – Yeah send Community Relations to Miller's Deli for a couple of orders.

W – Chief – You know Miller.

S – Oh I know what you mean. You go ahead. I don't drink while working, but it goes nice with corned beef.

W – Right Chief but, but

S – You don't have to salute when you leave Tom, just when you enter.

W –Right Chief, but..

S –Tom- you're not supposed to turn around and walk out – you're supposed to back out slowly.

W – Right Chief.

Tape inaudible – sounds like cursing.

Tape of Conversation 6 months later April 25, 1977

S – Herb Miller got one of our typewriters?

W – I told you about it Chief!

S – Yeah, probably between asking me if I wanted a tuna fish sandwich and a phone call.

W – No! Chief – you're wrong this time. It was between a phone call and corned beef.

S – Oh yeah, where did we get those sandwiches?

W – I think it was Millers Deli on 169th Street and Grand Concourse- I remember –

I had a beer with it. Community Relations picked them up for us.

S- Yeah about that time!

W- Right Chief its time again (phone rings)

S – 2 orders Tom.

W – Right Chief

S – Hello Doctor – Would you like to go to the Captains Luncheon with me. I'll pick you up at three quarters past eleven. Right – a Freudian slip. Make that 11-45. Right I have trouble seeing my watch. Hold it Doctor, I think someone's still here in my office, "Who's there?"

W – What's that Chief, I can't hear you – my ears, you know.
<Tape inaudible- mumbling.>

Sachson wanted me to develop a disaster plan for the Bronx – he didn't want a Yankee Stadium repeat. Between the required research and the writing of the plan, my time was filled for the next two weeks. We distributed the plan to all commands, requesting that all supervisory personnel have a working knowledge of it. Then I decided to have a little fun – let's test all the captains and above on the plan.

I created a disaster scenario – a plane hit a building in section 5 of Co-op City and crashed into Eastchester Bay after damaging the railroad bridge across the same bay.

Then, with the help of Lt. Cooney, we set-up a war room – four telephones, maps, directories, etc. Lt. Cooney would be the aide of the boss being tested. I had a police officer stationed in another room with a time chart and the telephone numbers to call with pre-determined problems. Lt. Cooney would answer the phone and either advise the candidate of the problem or tell him the rank and name of the caller and say "He wants to talk to you" and then be guided by the response.

This was more fun than the Christmas Party routine. We did our best to drive each and everyone of them crazy and to their credit, all but one did an excellent job. The feedback was fantastic – they loved it, claiming it was a great learning experience. To his credit, D.I. Ciccotelli was outstanding—the guy just loved being in charge.

Shortly thereafter, Sachson received his three-quarters pension and retired.

Chief Anthony Voelker replaced him. The chief had some lights installed in the hallway leading to his office – Green, Red and Yellow. Individuals approaching his office were to be guided by the traffic signals. Yes, I planned to use this as one of my subjects for my farewell performance at the Holidays/Promotion party in January of 1978.

But in May of 1977, other than my intense concern with the .44 caliber killer, I wanted one last shot at joining the National Football League. Yes, I was 42 years old, but I was a better than average kicker. In the Army, at Fort Benning, I had finished second in the punting competition to Yale Lary, who made quite a name for himself with the Detroit Lions.

I received the following letter:

Yonkers Raceway. Yonkers, N.Y. 10704
May 11, 1977

Dear Tom,
Please report to Yonkers Raceway on Saturday, May 14, at 3:20 p.m. for the Pittsburg Steelers punting and kicking tryout.
Enter at the Central Avenue gate and you may park in the preferred parking area.

Please bring your football cleats with you and be appropriately dressed with sweats or warm up pants.

If you have any questions please call this office.

Sincerely,
MICHAEL I, COHEN
PUBLICITY DIRECTOR

MIC:fk

In The Reporter Dispatch paper, of May 22, 1977, Bill Murphy, a staff writer in an article entitled, "Grid hopefuls get kick out of Steelers tryouts" wrote:

During aggravating wind conditions the athlete's alternated punts and field goals under the scrutiny of Haley, his assistant, Bill Nunn, and Steelers kicking coach, Paul Uram.

"What we're looking for is someone who can kick consistent field goals from 35-40 yards," stated Haley, burdened with numerous clipboards and stop watches. "If one of the punters can average 40 yards with a hang time of about 3.8 seconds, we'd also be interested in him."

One other potential Pittsburgher was busy trying to put George Plimpton to shame. Tom Walker, a 41 year-old New York City Police Captain was trying his hand (or rather his foot) at a short flirtation with the NFL. Walker recently authored "Fort Apache," a novel about the Bronx precinct where he works, and won $32,000 as a contestant on television's "$128,000 Question" quiz show. Was Walker serious about picking up where George Blanda left off?

"Look, I kicked a couple of 40-yard field goals before I pulled a muscle today. I have 20 years in with the force and I could retire tomorrow if the Steelers offered me a contract. It's something I always wanted to do, and let's face it, you can't win the lottery if you don't buy a ticket."

*   *   *

I also handled all departmental recognition requests for the entire borough. It kept me abreast of the violent happenings in the South Bronx. When Roger Smith was shot in the neck in the Four-one Precinct,

I upgraded his request for departmental recognition to a Combat Cross. Chief Braunstein (a nice man) said, "all he did was get shot."

Well, I loved the chief, but that remark sent me into orbit—everyone ran for cover.

The chief stuck to his position, but I honestly believed that he realized that his remark was in bad taste and belittled Smith's combat efforts.

However, most importantly, Roger survived the shooting.

*   *   *

On Wednesday, July 13, 1977, three lightning strikes at key locations created a sequence of events that by 9:36 p.m. E.S.T, The Con Edison power system had collapsed – New York City went dark. Subways, elevators, traffic lights, air conditioners, electric coffee pots, you name it – had stopped.

In a brutal heat wave in the middle of a financial crisis, with a psycho cutting little boy's penises off in Manhattan and the Son of Sam terrorizing The Bronx and Queens, this was the last thing a harried Mayor Beame needed. At that very moment, the doomed Mayor was in Co-op City making a campaign speech at a synagogue. He quipped, "This is what you get for not paying your bills".

In my townhouse across the Greenway, my wife lit candles, turned on the radio and turned to 10-10 WINS news. When it was reported that the blackout would last all night, I called the borough office for instructions. Report to your local precinct was the order that night.

Lacking a uniform, it was at the borough office, I pinned my shield onto my sports jacket and carefully drove to the 45th Precinct.

There were a few hot spots in the usually quiet Northeast Bronx precinct, but they were being adequately addressed by the precinct's commanding officer.

I manned the phones, listened to the chaos on the 8th Division radio from the 41st and 43rd Precincts, and kept in contact with the borough office.

The reports from the field were scary, disheartening and repugnant. It was truly a night of terror in the South Bronx,

An officer in the Four-one Precinct made a casual remark on the radio, "There seems to be an awful lot of Pontiacs out here tonight".

We learned late that 50 brand new Pontiacs had been stolen from Ace Pontiac in the west Bronx.

The borough wheel told me that Lt. Phil Romano had called looking for help. Romano was in the 46th Precinct on Fordham Road and Webster Ave in the middle of a riot – fires, looting, assaults. I knew Phil for years – he always managed to get into the middle of a fray.

A report from the lower sectors of the 4-3 Precinct reported that the looters were chanting, "Its Christmas time, its Christmas time."

In the 48 Precinct, $55,000 worth of furniture was stolen from a Tremont Avenue store.

Roving gangs wrenched iron shutters and gates from storefronts giving priority to businesses that featured clothing, TV's, jewelry and booze. When that task was completed, the looters menu shifted to food, furniture and drugs.

When he ordered the State of Emergency, Mayor Beame stated;

"We've seen our citizen's subjected to violence, vandalism, theft and discomfort. The blackout has threatened our safety and has seriously impacted our economy. We've been needlessly subjected to a night of terror. The cost when finally tallied will be enormous."

Every poor neighborhood, 31 in all, had been devastated – violence and plundering filled the night. Time reporter Mary Cronin touring the Four-one Precinct reported:

"Streams of black water from broken fire hydrants swept the residue of the looting into the middle of the street. In the new Fedco supermarket, shelves gleamed bare and white, while several inches of mashed produce, packages of squashed hamburgers, rivers of melted ice cream, and broken bottles covered the floor. The stench was overpowering. Up to 300 stores were cleaned out in the neighborhood, and the next morning sheets of plywood covered most of their smashed windows. Said Policeman John Fitzgerald: "There are only cops and crooks left here now." New York's massive show of police force, and the cops' restraint, helped keep the nightmare from becoming ever worse. The department mustered about 8,000 of its 26,000 person force, twice the number that would normally have been on duty."

25 hours after it started it was over. The lights flickered and then TV's blared, air conditioner hummed, and electric coffee pots perked – civilization had returned.

Until September 11, 2001, the 1977 blackout was the worst man-made catastrophe in 20th century New York City history.

The police made over 3,800 arrests – hundreds of officers had been injured, 18 seriously. The Fire Department had responded to 1,037 fires – 59 firefighters had been injured. Estimates of the damage ranged from 300 million to a billion. The level of civil discord exceeded the 1964 and 1968 riots. It was a disgrace.

A leader of the Puerto Rican United Front said, "You can't justify it". The headlines across the world reflected our shame.

The L.A. Times – "City's pride in itself goes dim in the blackout"
The Tokyo Mautichi – "Panic Grips New York"
Germany's Bild Zeitung – "New York's Bloodiest Night"
London's Daily Express – "The Naked City"

My friend Paul Burke, who had played Adam on the T.V. series "The Naked City", called me from his home on Palm Springs. He said something that I'll never forget! "If that can happen in the most generous and humane city in the world, what does that say about the human condition? "

I didn't have an answer.

*   *   *

No, I wasn't in suite 324 for the sixth game of the World Series between the Yankees and the Dodgers on October 18, 1977. And yes, I regretted not being there to watch Reggie Jackson smash 3 home runs to enable the Yankees to win the World Championship, 4 games to 2.

But I was at game 2 on October 12th, which was won by the Dodgers 6 to 1. However, since the Yankees won the series, that game should be of little interest, but it was. Once again, I must admit that I missed what did make it memorable. Why did I miss it? Because it happened on television. Howard Cosell supposedly uttered the words, "The Bronx is Burning"

The Facts:

An hour before the game began; a fire at P.S. #3, an abandoned elementary school near the stadium had started.

By 8 p.m. the 5 alarm fire had fully engulfed the building.

A review of the game tapes revealed the following:

It was a blustery night. In the bottom of the 1st inning, Keith Jackson mentioned the large size of the blaze.

Cosell replied that President Carter had visited the area yesterday. (The Four-one Precinct)

In the top of the second, aerial coverage picked up the huge blaze. Cosell told the viewers that the New York City Fire Department had a tough job to do in the Bronx.

Then in the bottom of the second, Cosell told the viewers that it was an abandoned building and no lives were in danger.

And for the rest of the game, there was no mention of the fire.

Why did I debunk this urban myth? Well, I was planning to write a chapter on The Bronx is Burning, but when my research revealed this information, I decided to do what Howard Cosell, despite his faults, always did – tell it like it is!

*   *   *

It was January 1978. It was time for my final roast of The Bronx's top brass past and present, at the annual holiday/promotion party. These affairs were attended by over 200 police personnel of all ranks. The common denominator among these folks was that they had all heard, generated or spread every piece of gossip that existed about their leaders.

So they knew that Chief Meehan had been transferred to The Bronx after his wife had an accident with his department vehicle.

They knew that Chief Sachson had received a three-quarters disability pension for glaucoma, and that I was seeking the same pension for an ear problem.

They knew that Tony Voelker had installed lights in the hallway leading to his office to control the traffic.

They knew the Tony Bouza had retired because of his misguided strategy on the 155th St, Macombs Dam Bridge.

They knew Chief Ray McDermott had been replaced by Tony Bouza and that now he was replacing Tony Voelker as Chief of the Bronx.

If they weren't aware of these events, my attempts at humor would fall flatter than it sometimes did.

And so it was that once again, Mario Caturo introduced me to a raucous crowd of meat eaters.

"Thank you, Mario. Before I start I'd like to take this opportunity to welcome Chief James Meehan to The Bronx (long pause) – he came to us by department vehicle". They loved that one.

"I see Chief Sachson over there.

Can you see me Chief?"

"I see you Walker", he yelled.

"What did you say? I replied, I can't hear you. The crowd went wild with delight.

"Chief Voelker, How are you tonight?'

He just nodded.

"Is that a red or green light Chief?" I probed.

The crowd roared, Tony shook his head. (I had a lot more for him but my instincts said, "You can't top that response.")

"Is Chief Bouza here tonight? I asked.

Someone pointed to a table.

"Hello Chief", I shouted "I hear they're remaking that World War 2 film in your honor."

Palumbo shouted, "What's it called?

"A Bridge too Far", I replied, committing a cardinal sin of roasters – laughing at one's own joke.

"Chief McDermott" I said, in the best brogue I could muster – that alone had the audience in stitches.

I was tempted to let it lie there, but I still hadn't told the joke.

"As you all know, Chief McDermott was replaced by a Tony and now he is replacing Tony. If there's one thing I can say about Chief McDermott it's that he is definitely not "Tony" (stylish). It got some chuckles.

I continued for another well received 15 minutes picking on the Inspectors and Deputy Inspectors.

The joke that got the best reception while roasting that group was:

"I hear that before he left Chief Voelker wanted to promote Deputy Inspector Ciccotelli. He tried but the Commissioner told him that there was no opening for an Emperor (that got the kind of laugh that says 'it's good that you're retiring') and so, I rode off into the sunset.

*   *   *

In April of 1978, my request for a three-quarters pension was denied.

On April 28, 1978, I retired from the N.Y.P.D. It had been a hellava ride – I loved it.

I've never been offered a Command, never made the NFL, never won $128,000 on a Quiz Show, never caught the Son of Sam, but thankfully, I've never been listed on that sacred wall in Police Headquarters as have so many wonderful young men and women.

So let's not diminish their heroism and accomplishment by spouting comparative statistics. Statistics bleed no blood, cry no tears, feel no pain, nor quell loved one's silent screams in the dark of night that whisper, "Oh, what might have been, what might have been." MyGod hold all them in the hollow of his hands.

And then President Leonard Lief granted me what Chief Tony Bouza wouldn't – a command. President Lief made me the Director of Security at Lehman College in The Bronx. (Now, that's when things really – Oh, well that's another story).

I prayed that the next time a serial bomber or killer appeared on the scene, that the powers-to-be would release the information to the public immediately.

I retired on April 28, 1978.

Less than a month later, on May 25, 1978, a bomb was placed on the University of Chicago campus (Netsch's Fortress).

It wasn't until December of 1994, 16 years later, that the F.B.I released to the New York Times information about a prolific serial bomber – he was called the Unabomber.

And so it goes!

Kids on Fox Street 1971

Simpson Street 1971

Dedication of Old 4-1 Precinct November 1997

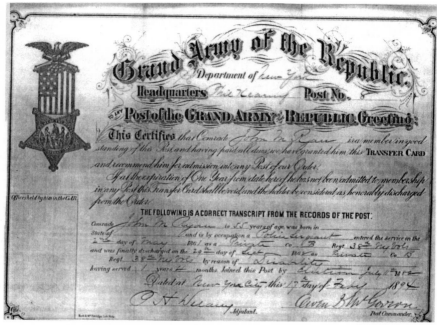

Transcript. Sgt. John M. Ryan, Co. B, 38th NY Vol. 1861
John was wounded at the Battle of Bull Run. He lost his 2 brothers in the Civil
War. Matthew was killed in the 1st battle of Big Bethel in PA. William was
killed serving under Admiral Farrigut at the Battle of Mobile Bay.

John M. Ryan Sgt. NYPD, 1898

John Ryan PTL NYPD, 1910

Howard Walker PTL NYPD, 1938 (Ret. Sgt.)

Howard Walker, Class Picture, Pelham Bay Park, 1938

Kathryn (Ryan) Walker and Howard Walker

Thomas J. Walker PTL NYPD, 1956 (Ret. Captain)

Standards
City Champs - 1954 - 1955 - 1956
Westchester County Champs 1956

Rear — Mike Caprara, Mgr., John Riley, Tom Walker, George Mittelstadt, George Reich, Bobby Middelstadt, John Kasara. Front — Lou Repetti, Joe Letizia, Babe Gabbamonte, Capt. Larry Pape, Billy Georges.

BABE GABBAMONTE, Capt.	BOBBY MITTELSTADT
MIKE CAPRARA, Mgr.	GEORGE MITTELSTADT
LARRY PAPE	JIM PULVERMILER
JOE LETIZIA	JOHNNY RILEY
TOM WALKER	GEORGE REICH
LOU REPETTI	FRANK CASUCCI
BILLY GEORGES	JOHN BRESCIA
ANDY HEINE	JOHN KASARA
DUKE FRANCESE	

Standards – 1956 Fast Pitch Champs Westchester, NY

Tom Walker & Mary Faherty – Engagement at Standard's Award Dinner –
Glen Island Casino – 1956

Thomas E. Walker – Navy Pilot

Thomas E. Walker – Swearing in Ceremony

John Walker, Mary Walker, Thomas E. Walker – St. Paddy's Day

John Walker, 1990 in Ireland – St. Patrick's Shrine

Mary Anne Walker – Police Officer, 1989 (Now a Lt.)

Mary Anne Walker and Partner, New Year's Eve 1992

Thomas J. Walker and Louis Palumbo (Ret. PLCL)

Tom & Mary Walker – Belmont Park, S.H. Silver Blaze

Ellen Walker (McDonagh), Mary Anne & Cathy Walker (Sisters)

Cathy, Mom & Dad at Wedding 1990

Cathy Walker (Right) Bridesmaid for Sue

Cathy, Ed Arrigoni, John Dearie & Helen Arrigoni at Yankee Stadium, Bronx, NY

Cast of "To Serve and Protect", NBC Mini-Series 1998

APPENDIX A

_____▼_____

This list includes the activity of all police officers assigned to the 41st Precinct from January 1, 1974 to October 31, 1974.

The activity of all detectives assigned to the 41 squad, anti-crime, or specialized duty is not included.

In order to evaluate this activity report, one should know the officer's assignment i.e. community affairs, chauffeur, summons man, patrol-officer, S.H. Security, T.S. operator, etc., etc.

January – October 1974

	ARREST	MOVERS	TAGS	SVC CALLS	PATROL
P.O. Frank J. Adams	1	25	73	343	377
P.O. John. F. Agnelli	19	36	55	516	279
P.O. William J. Angela	0	33	75	717	146
P.O. Roger Angwin	32	9	0	0	0
P.O. Cesar L. Aponte	44	0	0	0	0
P.O. Stephen Argenzio	0	12	18	235	63
P.O. Ralph A. Argiento	0	32	87	369	100
P.O. John Auriemma	0	45	211	539	384
P.O. Steven Bailey	0	15	9	46	8
P.O. Shirley Banton	1	25	67	486	102
P.O. Joseph J. Barile	5	71	40	462	125
P.O. James Bayreuther	5	12	26	284	60
P.O. Wayne H. Behnken	11	44	102	512	282
P.O. Robert H. Bietighofer	0	0	0	0	0
P.O. Charles Biener	17	31	42	513	284
P.O. Richard Biller	37	0	0	0	0
P.O. Robert Bilodeau	12	50	100	290	243
P.O. Raymond Bookman	5	14	60	150	50
P.O. Jack Brabant	1	42	59	725	123
P.O. Christopher Brannigan	14	27	74	277	89
P.O. Douglas Briel	5	16	35	356	170
P.O. John Brienza	1	78	178	813	123
P.O. Robert E. Broas	26	37	71	561	365
P.O. Nathaniel Brown	8	51	170	258	166
P.O. Louis Brutto	4	35	40	228	255

	ARREST	MOVERS	TAGS	SVC CALLS	PATROL
P.O. George A. Bunzel	2	17	39	369	124
P.O. Robert Butler	0	2	4	694	74
P.O. James J. Byrne	2	29	89	336	39
P.O. Joseph Byrne	4	38	54	499	114
P.O Thomas Byrns	66	35	14	225	138
P.O. Donald P. Cahill	0	0	37	0	0
P.O. John Carson	1	65	62	484	323
P.O. Michael A. Catalano	0	22	122	355	81
P.O. Joann Catanese	11	27	58	419	94
P.O. Robert J. Chapters	0	0	0	0	0
P.O. Nicholas J. Citrola Jr.	13	36	141	530	123
P.O. William J. Clifford	20	9	13	277	68
P.O. John Clohessy	0	0	0	0	0
P.O. Robert Coapman	27	18	11	323	97
P.O. Ralph J. Coffey	10	41	100	405	223
P.O. David B. Cohen	60	5	0	0	60
P.O Daniel J. Colasuonno	1	26	116	286	65
P.O. Neil Colello	6	57	130	781	142
P.O. Hector Collazo	1	32	139	585	148
P.O. Timothy Collins	13	33	139	486	85
P.O. Robert Collins	8	24	93	567	102
P.O. Raul Colon	0	0	0	0	0
P.O. William Conlan	2	80	88	560	109
P.O. Kenneth Connolly	5	29	63	461	86
P.O. William Connolly	2	81	260	422	88
P.O. Thomas F. Connors	9	161	49	630	101
P.O. Craig S. Contesini	2	24	50	318	65

	ARREST	MOVERS	TAGS	SVC CALLS	PATROL
P.O. John Corcoran	0	0	0	0	0
P.O. Vincent Cossa	10	38	174	1071	113
P.O. Charles D. Cossentino	7	46	114	857	126
P.O. Nicholas Costa	1	64	55	391	64
P.O. William Coyle	29	27	10	401	86
P.O. Francis P. Cunnane	0	0	0	0	0
P.O Walter Cyiowice	12	16	17	478	92
P.O. Marvin Dancey	7	45	103	587	102
P.O. Thomas D'Anna	0	0	0	80	8
P.O. Gregory Dardzinski	6	29	106	397	82
P.O. Reginald Davis	14	48	100	859	111
P.O. Eileen Degnan	2	37	97	448	174
P.O. Mario Delcastillo	13	33	107	555	105
P.O. Frank Delmas	9	26	53	469	103
P.O. Ralph N. Demaio	1	790	3736	186	140
P.O. Robert Dematas	56	10	7	0	0
P.O. Maurice Devito	0	20	42	282	56
P.O. Nicholas Dibrino	9	11	180	910	40
P.O. Thomas Diehl	0	0	0	0	0
P.O. Salvatore Dileo	10	45	66	667	132
P.O. Carl Dimarco	1	12	35	113	137
P.O. William Dinaso	1	55	65	373	126
P.O. Isidoro Diprima	1	29	70	694	144
P.O. George Dirscherl	2	55	208	654	150
P.O. John Dsiena	6	33	176	830	164
P.O. Peter J. Dispenza	5	33	52	304	134
P.O. Brian Donnelly	16	16	53	622	112

	ARREST	MOVERS	TAGS	SVC CALLS	PATROL
P.O. Michael D. Doyle	1	36	48	450	86
P.O. Theodore Dziedzic	12	72	137	659	111
P.O. Niles Edmead	21	31	61	430	108
P.O. Paul Elias	0	390	1416	52	153
P.O. John Elio	0	0	0	0	0
P.O. Murray Ellman	28	163	200	1073	171
P.O. Nestor Estefani	0	11	486	56	119
P.O. Robert A. Eugenia	2	0	84	534	80
P.O. Arthur G. Fabro	0	0	0	81	59
P.O. Thomas Falcone	0	7	26	115	25
P.O. Dominick Fargnoli	3	18	569	110	74
P.O William R. Feerick	0	0	0	0	0
P.O. Hugh Finnegan	1	30	62	319	82
P.O. Robert Fitzgerald	16	83	175	717	150
P.O. Thomas Fitzsimmons	6	11	132	159	42
P.O. Daniel Flannelly	10	39	73	548	120
P.O. Robert Fleming	13	2	0	0	0
P.O. William Fleming	11	34	75	550	108
P.O. Edward L. Fox	3	54	131	634	119
P.O. Richard Francis	3	46	118	710	147
P.O. Kenneth Frawley	2	23	66	208	58
P.O. James Frawley	0	0	0	0	0
P.O. Ralph L. Friedman	120	8	0	0	0
P.O. William R. Friend	13	73	145	652	117

	ARREST	MOVERS	TAGS	SVC CALLS	PATROL
P.O. Joseph Galvin	0	0	0	0	0
P.O. Patrick F. Galvin	2	31	55	334	75
P.O. John F. Giannetto	1	48	102	587	129
P.O. Lawrence Gierum	23	42	160	595	121
P.O. Robert Gillings	36	1	1	0	0
P.O. Stephen Glove	6	23	99	718	134
P.O. Martin R. Golberg	0	0	0	0	0
P.O. Mariano Gonzalez	2	52	80	595	141
P.O. Anthony J. Grecco	1	98	78	471	131
P.O. Mike Green Jr.	40	0	0	0	0
P.O. Henry A. Greene	0	66	22	116	133
P.O. John Greer	7	45	154	430	136
P.O. Donald G. Gregori	6	58	98	572	111
P.O. William Guillen	4	30	61	533	63
P.O. Daniel Haggerty	3	28	162	869	155
P.O. George Hankins	0	0	0	0	0
P.O. Kieran Harrington	5	462	1393	17	124
P.O. Kevin Hayden	10	51	68	570	170
P.O. James Hayes	1	46	115	562	137
P.O. Timothy I. Healey	3	19	85	358	138
P.O. Daniel Heidt	1	20	41	209	78
P.O. Neil Hellers	3	35	80	589	112
P.O. Frank Henry	20	45	93	572	84
P.O Lillian Hogans	1	8	21	260	60
P.O. Robert Hollingworth	7	103	186	865	148
P.O. Robert Holohan	3	21	82	624	93
P.O. George Hopter	1	34	60	536	83
P.O. Peter Hugger	7	57	140	590	120

	ARREST	MOVERS	TAGS	SVC CALLS	PATROL
P.O. William S. Hunter	1	82	142	430	149
P.O. Ernest Iarussi	0	0	0	0	0
P.O. Aniello Invitto	70	13	10	236	150
P.O. Richard James	0	0	0	0	0
P.O. Stephen Jefferson	8	49	69	0	0
P.O. Glenn T. Johnson	–	–	–	–	–
P.O. Francis E. Jones	13	27	42	311	63
P.O. James D. Jordan	5	32	74	904	127
P.O. Thomas H. Joseph	1	61	76	989	159
P.O. David Kalin	16	5	0	8	112
P.O. Stephen Kayne	4	13	41	872	132
P.O. Michael Keane	19	46	128	442	92
P.O. Charles F. Kee Jr.	2	121	298	422	362
P.O. Daniel Kelleher	7	34	139	667	118
P.O. Joseph G. Kelly	13	52	55	361	71
P.O. Kenneth J. Kelly	3	43	110	725	151
P.O. James Kenny	20	83	168	880	150
P.O. James P. Kerrigan	0	0	0	0	0
P.O. Henry V. Luba					
P.O. Alfred Kirms	0	503	1719	56	161
P.O. Ernest Kyle	2	27	125	824	141
P.O. Donato G. Landi	23	41	95	1002	154
P.O. Albert A. Laporta	0	0	0	0	0
P.O. Victor Larini	0	56	86	690	141
P.O. Wilson Lasalle	3	56	155	477	161
P.O. Frank J. Leonetti	2	87	217	758	159

	ARREST	MOVERS	TAGS	SVC CALLS	PATROL
P.O. Alfred J. Lisante Jr.	6	36	126	998	157
P.O. Kenneth List	0	872	4067	190	127
P.O. Frederick LLorens	0	0	0	0	0
P.O. Neil Lorenz	19	27	45	418	83
P.O. George McBean	1	3	0	793	86
P.O. Nathan McCain	53	0	0	0	0
P.O. Eugene McCarthy	3	18	30	237	47
P.O. James McDarby	3	0	0	65	11
P.O. James McDonagh	3	36	160	953	151
P.O. Carl G. McDougal	0	42	73	706	136
P.O. Robert Laino	–	–	–	–	–
P.O. Kenneth McGrath	9	51	193	878	143
P.O. John McGrath	8	18	147	588	133
P.O. John McHugh	10	54	120	736	120
P.O. Richard J. McLees	31	4	0	0	0
P.O. Lawrence McLoughlin	6	187	136	631	116
P.O. Patrick McGibney	–	–	–	–	–
P.O. John F. McShane	3	39	89	809	154
P.O. Kenneth Mahon	18	0	0	0	21
P.O. Salvatore Maida	4	31	35	395	77
P.O. Milton Maldonado	0	0	0	0	0
P.O. Kevin Malley	19	85	127	794	127
P.O. Julius Mannino	1	38	70	495	128
P.O. Anthony Marcantonio	3	37	138	566	109
P.O. John P. Marchessi	28	84	185	367	91
P.O. Richard Maresca	5	75	118	713	105
P.O. Michele V. Marino	8	49	27	715	134
P.O. Ralph Martino	0	17	47	225	55
P.O. Roy D. Martinosky	10	31	89	465	120
P.O. Philip L. Masi	9	91	203	546	91

	ARREST	MOVERS	TAGS	SVC CALLS	PATROL
P.O. Randolph Mayer	18	46	119	588	135
P.O. Richard F. Mayhew	4	29	103	1183	113
P.O. Mehrohoff	3	53	98	384	98
P.O. Timothy Mertens	0	13	77	404	110
P.O. James F. Meyers	17	43	128	758	139
P.O. Michael N. Moloney	10	55	144	675	139
P.O. William Mondore	7	25	42	390	81
P.O. Robert Montiel	8	33	79	718	143
P.O. William H. Moran	4	43	88	515	108
P.O. George Moravec	2	67	136	590	144
P.O. Frank N. Morelli	10	10	6	112	22
P.O. Michael Mortak	19	14	68	728	116
P.O. Arthur Murray	29	4	0	0	0
P.O. Thomas J. Murray	28	0	0	0	0
P.O. Danny Mutino	12	61	223	990	235
P.O. James P. Mylett	2	4	25	169	28
P.O. Ronald Nardello	2	39	102	423	116
P.O. Joseph Nardi	0	0	0	0	0
P.O. Jose Navarro	0	0	13	57	16
P.O. Octavio Narvaez Jr.	4	1	11	616	53
P.O. Richard Nestor	15	14	0	24	13
P.O. Brian J. Nicholson	4	25	204	1066	157
P.O. Angelo Norberto	5	50	97	460	96
P.O. Toby Novelli	9	33	75	324	91
P.O. Patrick F. O'Boyle	0	20	43	227	80
P.O. John O'Brien	4	16	33	277	64
P.O. Gerald O'Brien	42	32	121	492	87

	ARREST	MOVERS	TAGS	SVC CALLS	PATROL
P.O. Michael O'Connor	3	13	43	540	122
P.O. Patrick O'Connor	7	21	53	567	99
P.O. Kevin O'Grady	0	35	97	425	98
P.O. Fred Olsen	4	3	38	300	80
P.O. Daniel Opromolla	1	37	97	406	97
P.O. Mathew Orsi	58	29	90	529	67
P.O. Raphael Padilla	0	0	0	60	81
P.O. Charles Pagani	6	38	187	259	119
P.O. Mario T. Palmitto	3	31	146	109	109
P.O. William Paretti	8	37	103	740	139
P.O. Robert Parente	0	48	521	470	129
P.O. Carlos Pastrana	5	63	229	353	96
P.O Chester Paul	2	30	25	709	72
P.O. George S. Pearson	0	0	0	0	0
P.O. Gary Pellegrino	1	35	107	9	43
P.O. Frank T. Peneno	0	0	0	0	0
P.O. Steven Pepe	7	74	184	637	136
P.O. Robert Perez	5	22	51	524	152
P.O. Ronald Perks	17	1	1	8	8
P.O. George Peskar	1	494	1438	0	123
P.O. Peter J. Petrone	5	33	129	418	82
P.O. Patrick Phelan	36	18	34	414	128
P.O. Donald Player	14	39	60	302	69
P.O. William Pinamonti	1	31	708	856	150
P.O. Robert Poole	4	18	69	238	64
P.O. Michael W. Popp	0	0	0	0	0
P.O. Salvatore Porcino	4	28	49	434	86

	ARREST	MOVERS	TAGS	SVC CALLS	PATROL
P.O. Thomas Powers	8	17	44	553	123
P.O. Frank Racz	5	14	86	514	116
P.O. John Reggio	0	12	20	219	49
P.O. Charles C. Reid	2	32	91	201	154
P.O. James Reid	0	10	57	222	69
P.O. Joseph A. Rios	0	11	168	164	146
P.O. William Poche	5	32	75	370	111
P.O. Terrence Rocks	3	65	282	0	66
P.O. Amador Rodriguez	6	32	65	217	145
P.O. Evaristo Rodriguez					
P.O. Angel Roman	0	0	0	0	0
P.O. Max Rosado	0	0	0	0	0
P.O. Michael Rosco	1	29	67	322	98
P.O. Bernard Rosenberg	0	430	1535	0	63
P.O. Thomas J. Ross	3	13	9	233	61
P.O. Michael F. Roth	3	45	106	470	133
P.O. Wayne Rowe	10	41	72	517	89
P.O. Michael Rowland	2	51	102	718	143
P.O. Lester Rudnick	11	56	87	673	127
P.O. Timothy Ryan	6	17	46	309	60
P.O. Frank Sabatino	4	43	82	458	127
P.O. Luis Salgado	9	69	117	737	106
P.O. Robert Salters	4	40	96	297	106
P.O. Carmelo Santana	6	10	23	262	135
P.O. John Santos	14	53	152	709	155
P.O. Jose F. Santiago	0	5	196	103	148
P.O. Frank Schmitt	8	38	70	610	120
P.O. Paul Schmucker	16	101	159	789	144

	ARREST	MOVERS	TAGS	SVC CALLS	PATROL
P.O. Lawrence Schurek	4	56	59	390	85
P.O. Arnold D. Schwartz	–	–	–	–	–
P.O. Robyn Schwartz	7	52	113	492	96
P.O. Steven Schwartz	17	12	37	736	123
P.O. Ignacio Serrano	5	49	140	622	138
P.O. Anthony D. Sesack	2	25	82	436	129
P.O. Salvatore Sgarlata	0	0	0	0	0
P.O Ernest Sierra	0	12	63	459	112
P.O. Martin L. Silverman	6	32	66	517	103
P.O. John T. Smith	0	0	0	0	0
P.O. Roger G. Smith	24	11	11	369	41
P.O. Robert Soreco	3	22	39	511	114
P.O. Robert L. Soule	2	9	29	623	131
P.O. William Spero	60	0	0	0	21
P.O. James J. Squillace	2	36	94	946	159
P.O. Joseph Spagnuolo	16	41	79	387	127
P.O. Karl Stigell	7	108	443	102	143
P.O. Richard Stilwagen	3	37	179	357	93
P.O. Samuel Strassfield	0	0	0	0	0
P.O. Luis Suarez	8	82	126	504	110
P.O. Francis X. Sullivan	0	107	29	189	147
P.O. John J.Sullivan	0	16	29	19	13
P.O. Richard Sullivan	4	44	92	955	138
P.O. Patrick Talbot	4	38	163	945	154

	ARREST	MOVERS	TAGS	SVC CALLS	PATROL
P.O. Frederick Tarantino	1	14	3067	489	102
P.O. Nelson A. Thau	58	5	0	0	64
P.O. Charles Thornberg	0	0	0	0	0
P.O. Harold E. Tibbetts Jr.	3	57	119	605	130
P.O. Rocco Tortorello	0	15	45	176	48
P.O. Richard J. Turdely	0	69	176	539	85
P.O. Carroll W. Tyler	0	0	0	0	0
P.O. Anthony C. Valenti	0	8	26	277	47
P.O. Milton Vanleuvan	13	48	261	666	125
P.O. Gilberto Vargas	1	800	1472	1	128
P.O. Wilfred Vazquez	4	76	164	781	157
P.O. Alejandro Vega Concepcio	3	32	88	913	97
P.O. Robert Vecchiarello	2	113	624	0	157
P.O. Robert Verone	2	40	70	757	75
P.O. John F. Vietro	0	0	0	0	0
P.O. Joseph Viggiani	4	29	116	708	132
P.O. Herman Visser	2	15	49	302	118
P.O. James Waldron	0	32	68	454	122
P.O. Richard W. Wellington	2	38	82	428	127
P.O. James P. Walsh	1	6	13	82	16
P.O. William Walsh	0	15	7	111	43
P.O. Nero Wells	5	28	372	0	62

	ARREST	MOVERS	TAGS	SVC CALLS	PATROL
P.O. Donald A. Wenz	1	94	184	936	125
P.O. Kenneth Wilkinson	17	39	60	587	138
P.O. George Williams	2	14	26	391	124
P.O. John J. Wekerle	5	10	26	278	62
P.O. Philip Wohlfert	1	20	68	412	109
P.O. Stanley Wojcik	7	27	70	361	93
P.O. Martin Zinkand	0	0	0	31	0
Anti- Crime and Special duty Detective					
41 Det. Squad names not included					
Det. Irwan M. Black					
Det. Lawrence Donegan					
Det. Edwin Fennell					
Det. Robert S. Gardiner					
Det. William J. Gerhardt					
Det. Paul J. Gornie Jr.					
Det. Lawrence Hinrichs					
Det. John k. Jacobsen					
Det. Frank Macchio					
Det. William C. Rath					
Det. Alan Sperling					
Det. Lonny Spivey					
Det. Douglas Vassilatos					
Det. George W. Wieber					
Det. James J. Finn					
Det. John Flanagan					
Det. Robert W. Ulich					

APPENDIX B

▼

1974

**ANNUAL
REPORT
41st PRECINCT**

**Joseph G. Sampson
Deputy Inspector
Commanding Officer**

Thomas J. Walker
Joseph W. Slattery
Executive Captain
Executive Captain

1974 ANNUAL REPORT

41ST PRECINCT

Every organization, large and small, issues annual reports which denote the gains that have been made during the past year, and indicates the direction in which the organization must move during the new year to increase productivity and profit. Since we are a municipal service unit, we must stress not only productivity but customer contentment with our service. The following information should provide you with some sense of our accomplishments and also help to focus your attention on several critical areas, where improvement is desirable.

1.   The most important area in which we are involved is crime. Listed below are the 1973 figures as compared with the 1974 ones. As you can see we did a great job in the categories of Robbery, Burglary and Assault. (Complaints down, arrests up). In 1975 we must continue to give our maximum efforts in these areas while improving in the G.L.A and purse snatch categories. I think that these figures show that the men and women of the 41 are doing an admirable and highly effective job in fighting serious crime.

	1974		1973	
	COMPLAINTS	ARRESTS	COMPLAINTS	ARRESTS
Homicide	77	4	87	4
Rape	121	38	162	51
Robbery	1761	413	2004	333
Assault	903	407	1032	239
Burglary	3441	796	4013	695
G.L.A	770	242	927	357
G/L Purse	232	3	175	6

2.   Bribery Arrests – We ranked #1 in the borough and city again this year with twenty one (21) arrests. Last year our nineteen (19) arrests led the field. Another note of encouragement was that our corruption complaints decreased by 19.7% during 1974. This was the third (3rd) best decrease in the borough. Keep up the good work. I.A.D. informed us that our Corruption Program was excellent.

3. Arson Arrests – One of the big problems in this precinct are fires, many deliberately started for various reasons, which endangered innocent people and caused extensive damage. We have made twenty-nine (29) arson arrests this year and have saved hundreds of people from harm through fire rescues. There is little doubt in my mind that we rate #1 in both these categories. Your concern for these innocent victims and your enforcement action in this area is commendable.

4. Traffic Safety – The number of accidents decreased from 1,945 in 1973 to 1,823 in 1974. This year we rank #1 in the borough with an Accident Enforcement Index of 29.79. Last year we were #2 with an index of 10.13. We ranked #1 in the borough this year for the number of moving summonses issued. Our summons figures are listed below:

	1974	1973
Personal	22,550	20,286
Parking	59,643	52,961

What makes these figures even more impressive is the considerable gains made during a period of declining population. Keep it up.

5. Warrant Enforcement

	1974	1973
Received	798	766
Arrests	116	79

Our warrant enforcement improved greatly during 1974, but we slipped from #1 in the borough in 1973 to #2 in the borough in 1974. Nevertheless, an outstanding job, keep it up.

6. Intelligence – I was informed by the Intelligence Division that we <u>rank #1</u> in the Borough as to both the quantity and quality of our intelligence information. This is a tribute to all the men in the field. Keep the information coming. Police Officer DeVito is the first to admit his dependence on you.

7. Auto Recovery Unit – The Auto Recovery Unit made one hundred and sixty four (164) arrests this year. Good Work fellows.

8. Anti-Crime – Once again Anti-Crime proved why they are the best in the city. City wide gave our unit eighteen (18) Excellent and six (6) Goods of a possible twenty four (24) Excellent.

	1974	1973
Arrests	1,251	1,146

These were quality arrests. Two members, Cohen and Spero, were made detectives as a result of their outstanding work. Thomas Murray was promoted to sergeant. Stanley Gamb, a graduate of Anti-Crime, also got the shield.

Tragically, Kenny Mahon, who also had a gold shield in his future, made the supreme sacrifice for the people of New York on December 28, 1974. There is no earthly way to measure this loss, only in heaven can these things be measured. How do you measure a friendly smile, a kind word, a pat on the back, a dry joke, a helping hand? We all knew Kenny as a man, and the death of any man you know diminishes you. We all know Kenny as a good man, and the untimely death of a good man is always a tragedy. We all knew Kenny as a good man and a good cop, so surely this tragedy diminishes not only us, but all peace loving people in the city. He made a difference, you all do!

9. Line of Duty Injuries – A recent report rated us as #2 in the city re: assaults on officers. Ranked #1 in shoot-outs. The total number of line of duty injuries (assaults, accidents) decreased from one hundred and ninety (190) in 1973 to one hundred and eighty four (184) in 1974. Let's hope the trend continues.

10. Department Recognitions

E.P.D.'s	205
M.P.D.'s	117
Commendations	61
Exceptional Merit	17
Honorable Mention	12
Combat Cross	3 (plus several pending)
Medal of Honor	1 (pending)

These figures speak for themselves.

11. Response Time – Best in Zone 2 for 1974. We have improved by one (1) minute from 1973 to reach a yearly average of twenty eight (28) minutes. Continue improvement is our goal. Our radio runs were fifth in the Borough behind the 44, 42, 48 and 43 Precincts.

12. Command Discipline

1974	1973
154	171

A decrease in the need for disciplinary action is a positive thing. A self-disciplined force is highly desirable. Our sergeants and lieutenants have helped to create this positive atmosphere.

13. Civilian Complaints

1974	1973
90	80

An increase in these complaints has caused us concern. While we realize that many of these complaints are unavoidable, an increase of 12.5 % is not to be treated lightly. We have started an educational program in this area and request that each of you examine your handling of situations to help us to reduce these complaints in 1975.

14. Community Relations and Crime Prevention – Our Community Relations and Crime Prevention personnel continue to provide a superior service to the community. They were given a rating of "Excellent" by the Inspections Division for 1974. You're doing great job fellows.

15. P.I.U. – During 1974 the 41 squad conducted 2,996 investigations which resulted in five hundred and eight (508) arrests and three hundred (300) other cases were closed with results. Police Officer John Mahoney was promoted to sergeant and Detective David Dean retired. Keep up the good work.

16. Other Advancements
    P.O. Donald Wenz to Sergeant
    P.O. Jimmy Walsh to Sergeant
    P.O. Stanley Wojcik to Sergeant
    P.O. John Edmondson to Lieutenant

In assessing our situation for 1974, one is left with the feeling, that the men of this precinct are doing a great job under trying conditions. In line with this evaluation we are going to make a recommendation that the precinct be considered for a Unit Citation. Chief Bouza has assured us that he will give it serious consideration. Once again, I want to extend my sincere thanks to all uniformed and civilian members of the command for their outstanding efforts to make the 41st Precinct number one in the borough.

APPENDIX C

▼

<u>January 14, 1976 Roster of Fort Apache</u>

RANK	NAME
<u>RANK</u>	<u>NAME</u>
CAPT	CLIFFORD
D.I	SAMPSON, JOS. G
CAPT	SLATTERY, JOS.W
CAPT	WALKER, THOM
LT	BARRON, JOS. J
LT	CORRIGAN, ROBERT E
LT	MARKMAN, MICHAEL P
LT	MAZZARULLI, SALVATORE J
LT	MONTAGNINO, JOS. A. JR
LT	NIMMO, ROBERT F

Four-one P.I.U.

RANK	NAME
DET's.	ARNETT, ALFRED
	BULLARD, AUDLEY
	CRUZ, ORLANDO
	DOYLE, ROBERT
	DUFFY, BERNARD
	FOWLER, KENNETH
	GIBLIN, WM.
	HART, HENRY Jr.
	JOHNSON, GLENN
	JONES, ROMAN
	MAHON, DAVID
	ROBERTS, GENE
	SAVAGE, ROGER
	SILVERSTEIN, JAY
	STRAINING, JOHN
	WILLIAMS, ARTHUR J

SGT	ALVAREZ, THOM. C
SGT	BARONE, VINCENT. W
SGT	BATTAGILA, JOHN P
SGT	CULLINEY, PHILIP P
SGT	DIBIASE, JOHN
SGT	DOONAN, WM. W
SGT	GAUGHAN, EDWARD
SGT	GISONNI, MARION J
SGT	HOUSTON, THOM. P
SGT	HUGHES, CHAS. W
SGT	MASON, ALFRED A
SGT	McCAFFREY, THOM, P
SGT	McCULLOUGH, EDWARD B
SGT	MENNON, ROBERT G
SGT	PURTILL, JOHN J
SGT	SAGESSER, JOHN H
SGT	SAVINO, VINCENT
SGT	SEIGNIOUS, ROBERT
SGT	STOKER, JOHN A
SGT	ST. ONCE, DENNIS W
SGT	SULLIVAN, DANIEL T

GOLD SH. DET's

DONEGAN, LAWERENCE
FENNELL, EDWIN
FINN, JAMES J
FLANAGAN, JOHN
GARDINER, ROBERT S
GERHARDT, WM J
GORNIE, PAUL J. Jr
HINRICH, LAWERENC
JACOBSEN, JOHN K

MACCHIO, FRANK
NIELSEN, JOHN
RATH, WM. C
SPERLING, ALAN
ULICH, ROBERT W
VASSILATOS, DOUGLAS
WIEBER, GEO. W

P.O'S

ADAMS, FRANK J

AGNELLI, JOHN F, Jr.

ANGELA, WM. J

ANGWIN, ROGER A

APONTE, CESAR L

ARGIENTO, RALPH

AURIEMMA, JOHN F

AYALA, JESUS R

BARATTINI, PETER

BARILE, JOS. A

B AYREUTHERM JAMES E

BEHNKEN, WAYNE H

BILLER, RICHARD J

BILODEAU, ROBERT J

BRABANT, JACK J

BRANNIGAN, CHRISTOPHER

BRIEL, DOUGLAS C

BROAS, ROBERT E

BROWN, NATHANIEL C Jr

BRUTTO, LOUIS

BUNZEL, GEO. A

BUTLER, ROBERT E

BYRNE, JAMES

BYRNE, JOS. A

B YRNS, THOMAS J

CABERA, LORENZO

CAHILL, DONALD

CATALANO, MICHEAL A

DAVENPORT, CHAS. H

DANCEY, MARVIN

DARDINSKI, GREGORY

DAVIS, REGINALS L

DELMAS, FRANK

DEMAIO, RALPH

DEMATAS, ROBERT P

DEVITO, MAURICE

DIBRINO, NICHOLAS Jr.

DIEHL, THOM. J

DILEO, SALVATORE G

DIMARCO, CARL M

DINASO W.M. J

DIPRIMA, ISIDORO N

DISIENA, JOHN

DISPENZA, PETER J

DONNELY, BRAIN T

DOYLE, MICHAEL D

DZIEDZIC, THEODORE

EDMEAD, NILES A

ELIAS, PAUL

ELIO, JOHN R

ELLMAN, MURRAY

FABBRO, AURTHER G

FANNING, DENNIS P

FARGNOLI, DOMINICK

FARNWORTH, JOHN J

FARRELL, GEO. F

CHARTERS, ROBERT

CITROLA, NICHOLAS J, Jr

CLAVIN, MICHAEL J

CLIFFIRD, WM C

CLOHESSY, JOHN P

COLASUONIC, DANIEL J

COLELLO, NEIL J

COLLINS, TIMOTHY N

COLLINS, WM. T

CONLAN, WM, J

CONNOLLY, KENNETH T

CONNOLLY, WM. J

CONNOR, KEVIN M

CONNOR, THOMAS F

CO NTESINI CRAIG S

CORCORAN, JOHN

COSSA, VINCENT H

COSTA, NICHOLAS P

COYLE, WM. R

CURLEY, ROBERT J

CYTOWICZ, WALTER Z

FEERICK, WM. R

FERNANDEZ, ALFRED

FINNEGAN, HUGH S

FITZGERLD, ROBERT G

FLEMING, ROBERT F

FLEMING, WM. J

FOX, EDWARD L

FRANCIS, RICHARDS

FRAWLEY, KENNETH J

FRIEND, WM. R

GALVIN, JOS.M

CALVIN, PATRICK F

GIANNETTO, JOHN F

GIERUM, LAWERENCE

GILLINGS, ROBERTS

GIOVE, STEPHEN J

GONZALEZ, MARIANO E

GRECCO, ANTHONY

GREEN, MIKE Jr.

GREENE, HENRY A

GREER, JOHN A

GREGORI, DONALD

GRIBBEN, JAMES R

GRIFFIN, CLARENCE A

P.O.'s		
HAGGERTY, DANIEL H		MASI, PHILLIP L
HANKINS, GEO. W		MAYER, RANDOLPH T
HARRINGTON, KIERAN F		MAYHEW, RICHARD F
HARTIGAN, DENNIS J		MEHROFF, BRAIN
HAYDEN, KEVIN J		MERTENS, TIMOTHY A
HEALEY, TIMOTHY L		MEYERS, JAMES F
HEIDT, DANIEL M		MOLONEY, MICHAEL
HOTTER, GEO. T Jr.		MONTIEL, ROBERT L
HUGGER, PETER		MORAN, WM. H
		MORAVEC, GEO. W
INVITTO, ANIELLO S		MORELLI, FRANK N
		MORTAK, MICHAEL
JEFFERSON, STEPHEN M		MULLER, ROBERT
JOSEPH, TOM. H		MURRAY, ARTHUR
		MUTINO, DANNY G
KALIN, DAVID J		MYLETT, JAMES P
KAYNE, STEPHEN,		
KEANE, MICHAEL L		NARDELLO, RONALD
KEE, CHAS. F. Jr		NARDI, JOS. J
KELLY, JOS. G		NARVAEZ, OCTAVIO N
KELLY, KENNETH J		NESTOR, RICHARD F
KENNY, JAMES P		NICHOLSON, BRAIN J
KIRMS, ALFRED		NIXON, CHAS. R
KYLE, ERNEST R		NOVELLI, TOBY G

LAINO, ROBERT J	O'BOYLE, PATRICK F
LANDI, DONATO G	O'BRIEN, JOHN J
LEONETTI, FRANK	O'CONNOR, JOHN B
LISANTI, ALFRED J. Jr	O'CONNOR MICHAEL G

LIST, KEENETH J

LLORENS, FREDERIC J

LOPEZ, ROLANDO R

LORENZ, NEIL L

LUBA, HENRY V

McBEAN, GEO. H

McCAIN, NATHAN M

McCARTHY, EUGENE F

McCARTHY, TIMOTHY

McDARBY, JAMES F

McDONAGH, JAMES C

McDOUGAL, CARL G

McGRATH, JOHN J

McGUIRE, CHRISTOPHER

McHUGH, JOHN P

McLEES, RICHARDS J

MCLOUGHLIN, LAWRENCE

McSHANE, JOHN F

MAHONEY, EDWARD J

MALDANADO, MILTON M

MALLEY, KEVIN P

MARCANTONIO, ANTHONY V

MARCHESI, JOHN P

MARESCA, RICHARD P

MARINO, MICHELE V

MARTINO, RALPH

O'CONNOR, PATRICK A

ODIOT, PETER E Jr

O'GRADY, KEVIN B

OLSEN, FRED A. Jr

OPROMOLLA, DANIEL

PADILLA, RAPHAEL

PALMIOTTO, MARIO T

PARCHEN, ROBERT J

PARENTE, ROBERT J

PARETTI, WM K

PASCALICCHIO, JAMES

PASTRANA, CARLOS

PATTERSON, CHAS, F Jr.

PAUL, CHESTER L

PEARSON, GEO. S

PELLEGRINO, GARY

PENENO, FRANK T

PEREFRIN, ANTHONY P

PERKS, RONALD

PESKAR, GEO. W

PETRONE, PETER J

PHELAN, PATRICK M

PINAMONTI, JOHN A

PLAYER, DONALD A

PORCINO, SALVATORE

POWERS, THOM. J

RACZ, FRANK JR		VALENTI, ANTHONY C. Jr.
REESE, KENNETH A		VAN LEUVAN, MILTON
REID, CHAS. C		VARGAS, GILBERTO

REID, JAMES M		VAZQUEZ, WILFRED
ROCHE, WM. F		VECCHIARELLO, ROBERT
ROCKS, TERRENCE A		VEGA-CONCEPTION, ALEJANDRO
RODRIGUEZ, AMADOR		VERONE, ROBERT
ROSENBERG, BERNARD S		VIETRO, JOHN F
ROSS, THOM. J		VIGGIANI, JOS.
ROTH, MICHAEL F		VIGGIANO, FRANK X. Jr
ROWE, WAYNE G		VISSER, HERMAN
ROWLAND, MICHAEL A		
RUDNICK, LESTER A		WALDRON, JAMES P
RYAN, TIMOTHY P		WATSON, GRANVILLE F
		WEKERLE, JOHN J
SABATINO, FRANK J		WELLINGTON, RICHARD E
SLAGADO, LUIS		WILLIAMS, GEO. L
SALTERS, ROBERT L		WOHLFERT, PHILIP Jr
SANTANA, CARMELO		
SANTOS, JOHN J		ZINKAND, MARTIN J
SCHMITT, FRANK A		
SCHMUCKER, PAUL W		P.A.A'S
SCHWARTZ, ARNOLD D		ARCHER, WARREN
SCHWARTZ, STEVVEN M		BASS, PATTI
SERRANNO, IGNACIO		BATEAU, MARY L
SGARLATA, SALVATORE R		BATTLE, DAVID
SMITH, JOHN T		BENNET, BERNARD
SMITH, ROGER G		BLUMM, SARA
SORECO, ROBERT J		DANCEY, DENISE
SOULE, ROBERT L		DEAN, SHIRLEY
SPAFGNUOLO, JOS. A		HADDOCK, ROSEMARY
SQUILACE, JAMES J		JACKSON, DIANE
STARKEY, GILBERT M		JEFFRIES, FRANCES
STIGEIL, KARL C		JESSAMY, SYLVIA

STILWAGEN, RICHARD		KITT, DONIEL
STRASSFIELD, SAMUEL		POPE, BEVERLY
SUAREZ, LUIS L		PEREZ, ANIBAL
SULLIVAN, FRANCIS X		PLOTNICK, MORRIS
SULLIVAN, RICHARDS P		REGAN, PATRICK
		ROBERSON, SHAREN
TALBOT, PATYRICK J		ROBINSON, FRANCINE
TARATINO, FREDERICK P		SHINNICK, MARGARET
THAU, NELSON A		SMITH, EARL S
THORNBERG, CHAS		
TIBBETTS, HAROLD E Jr.		CUSTODIAN
TORTORELLO, ROCCO F		LOMAX, JOE N
TURDELY, RICHARD		VALLE, JOE
TYLER, CARROLL W		

CPSIA information can be obtained at www.ICGtesting.com
Printed in the USA
LVOW11s2238170215

427246LV00001B/154/P